Hey Joseph!

A Complete
Lenten Program

Arley K. Fadness

CSS Publishing Company, Inc., Lima, Ohio

HEY JOSEPH!

For more information about CSS Publishing Company resources, visit our website at www.csspub.com or e-mail us at custserv@csspub.com or call (800) 241-4056.

Cover design by Chris Patton
ISBN 0-7880-2344-6

PRINTED IN U.S.A.

To my puppeteer clown friends,
Ed and Estelle Swanson,
also known as Papa and Mama Pogo,
who are always a hoot and inspiration

To my brother-in-law Dan Gudahl,
wife Ana and niece Jennifer,
and their phenomenal commitment
to Third World Development

Table Of Contents

Author's Preface

Children, teens, moms, dads, grandparents, and folks from all five generations grew in faith and made new connections during the Lenten season at Messiah Lutheran Church in North Mankato, Minnesota, around the theme, "Hey Joseph!"

The GI and Silent generation's ladies (b. 1900-1945), along with a few Baby Boomers (b. 1946-1964), made quilts from eleven inch square patterned cloth blocks, which were brought and presented in the worship by the Millennials (b. 1982-present).

Gen Xers (b. 1965-1981) and Boomers acted out the "drama-lies" (drama and homilies intermingled) while the pastor preached one or two homilies based on the Old Testament Joseph's life and adventures.

John Ylvisaker's "Joseph's Dream," the selected ballad for the series, proved an upbeat story summary each week.

This music cannot be reproduced or copied without written permission from John Ylvisaker. John may be contacted at Box 321, Waverly, Iowa 50677-0321; phone: 319-352-4396; fax: 319-352-0765; or e-mail: ylvisaker@kca.net.

Children brought nonperishables for Joseph's Granary. Grandparents taught the children how to do five social ministry projects and gave an object to illustrate each ministry. For example, for Native American ministry, the children received a dream catcher.

Hey Joseph! illustrates that during Lent and other settings, the multigenerational approach can't be beat!

Introduction

Hey Joseph! features the story of Joseph from Genesis 37:1—50:21.

Hey Joseph! is an interactive, intergenerational "Dramily" (drama and homily) designed for Lenten midweek worships that utilizes homilies interwoven into dramas that recasts and retells the Joseph story from the Old Testament.

The six weeks midweek production sets the stage for the story of Jesus' suffering and death in Holy Week.

The sanctuary becomes the stage.

The sanctuary resembles a theatre in the round with pastors, worship leaders, actors, and worshipers all playing significant roles in the learning/worship dramily.

At least three age levels of actors are employed. Actors "freeze" during mini-teaching homilies that are interspersed within the drama. Congregational response is invited and encouraged.

Hey Joseph! features one of the most action-packed stories in the Old Testament. It has contemporary relevance in that it deals with family squabbles, favoritism, sibling rivalry, hatred, jealousy, lies, innocence, falsely accused, dreams with meanings, prophecies, God's guidance and providence, confession and forgiveness, family reconciliation and healing, trust and shalom.

The theme song "Joseph's Dream" by John Ylvisaker tells the Joseph story in song.

Nonperishable food may also be brought to stock "Joseph's Granary" in preparation for the "famine." The "granary" can be set out for all to view and see how it fills up throughout the Lenten season.

Fasting and prayer are encouraged from time to time during the Lenten season.

Schedule

Oh, Joseph, you are so much like us! As we get acquainted with you, we recognize ourselves. You, Joseph, son of Jacob and Rachel, with many siblings, went through it all — favoritism, family squabbles, sibling rivalry, jealousy, hatred, lies, innocence, false accusations, dreams with meanings, prophecies, God's guidance and providence, confession and forgiveness, family reconciliation, healing, renewed trust, and shalom.

You, Joseph, are every man in so many ways.

Thank you, Joseph, we, too, will remember, "... God intended it for good, in order to preserve a numerous people, as he is doing today" (Genesis 50:20).

JOSEPH'S DREAM

John Ylvisaker

When we need a Re- deem- er, God will send us a dream- er!

1. Jo- seph dreamed of pow- er,
2. Is- ra- el was shak- en,
3. Re- con- cil- i- a- tion,

coat looked like a flow- er, In the zer- o hou- r,
land was al l for- sa- ken, Sil- ver cup was ta- ken,
bles- sing of a na- tion, Time for cel- e- bra- tion,

Jo- seph's dream came true!
Jo- seph's dream came true!
Jo- seph's dream came true!

We Need Bread For The World

We need bread, bread, bread for the world, bread, bread,

bread for the world____, bread, bread, bread for the world to-day ____

Sing it loud. ____

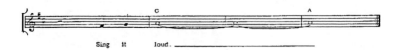

Sing it loud. ____

Additional Verses: "We need: love, peace,
hope, grace, truth ...."

Lenten Vespers
"Hey Joseph!"

Prelude

Welcome

Versicle *(cantor ... congregation echo)*

Lenten Hymn *(to be announced)*

Confession And Absolution

Leader: Let us confess our sins to God in the presence of one another. *(Silence for reflection and contrition)*
Lord God, our lover and forgiver.

All: **Listen to our failures in love and life. We admire virtues such as caring, community, and concern, but instead we practice anger, jealousy, and hatred. We applaud family, church, and God, but practice selfishness, distrust, and deception.**

We desire kindness, forgiveness, and gentleness, but find ourselves in bondage to sin.

Forgive the sins of our fallen state. Wipe away the stain caused by broken promises and restore us to true life in Jesus Christ our Lord.

Leader: This is how God shows love and forgiveness for us. Jesus came. Jesus lived. Jesus died. Jesus rose again. By him your sins are forgiven.

All: **Amen.**

13

Lesson(s)

Responsory   "Be Thou My Vision"

Prayer

Theme Song   "Joseph's Dream"
Used by permission John Ylvisaker, Waverly, Iowa

The Dramily   *"Hey Joseph!"*

Offering

Children's Time

Prayers
Leader: Let us pray. Gracious God,
All: **In the abundance of your steadfast love, give to us a
          vision for Shalom in all of life — that broken — we
          may be healed, alienated — we may be reconciled,
          discouraged — we may know gladness of heart. Bring
          together husbands and wives, children and parents,
          families and nations. Bond the human family together
          by your redemptive love. Empower all to seek justice.
          Make us stewards of this earth and bearers of good
          news in Christ our Lord. Amen.**

Benediction

Lenten Hymn

Postlude

Ash Wednesday

Shalom Unravels
Genesis 37:1-36

Characters
    Narrator
    Bilhah
    Joseph (teenager)
    Zilpah
    Ten Brothers
    Jacob
    Signbearer (nonspeaking)

Props
    Palm trees made from PVC pipe (see page 101 for a diagram), tent backdrop, water jars, robe, box, "Shechem" sign, "Dothan" sign

Narrator: This Lenten season we will see, hear, and experience that great story of Joseph and his brothers as recorded in Genesis chapters 37-50. I invite you to read this classic drama on your own and then come worship with us, learn, and enjoy.

(music intro)

Scene 1
(Bilhah, Zilpah, and Joseph are busy with chores and duties around the tent)

Bilhah: Hey, Joseph! *(louder)* Hey, Joseph!

Joseph: Yes, Ma'am. What is it?

Bilhah: Help Zilpah and me lift this water jar, if you please.

Joseph: Okeydokey. *(they lift and do some chores together)*

Bilhah: There, that's better. My fibromyalgia has been acting up lately so I appreciate your good help Joseph.

Joseph: No problem, Bilhah. Ma'am. Ahh, ahh ... *(stammers, stutters)*

Bilhah: What is it? Spit it out.

Joseph: While I'm helping you around the place I've got something to tell you.

Zilpah: *(hard of hearing)* You've got something to *sell*?

Joseph: No, No! *(Joseph and Bilhah laugh)* Zilpah, Ma'am, I was just saying I have something to tell! Tell! Not sell! *(all laugh good naturedly)*

Bilhah: Well — what is it, Joseph? I'm holding my breath.

Joseph: I'm, I'm telling Dad on my brothers.

Zilpah: You're sad like the others? *(looks puzzled)*

Bilhah: No, No, Zilpah, he said he's going to tell Dad on the brothers.

Zilpah: Oh? Well — what is it? What is it?

Joseph: Well, this is what's happening. You know ... *(fades out so that the audience cannot hear except when a brother's name is mentioned)* Reuben ... and then blah blah ... and Judah ... and Naphtali ... and ... Zebulun ... Issachar ... Asher ... Levi ... Simeon.

Bilhah: Rat ... rat ... rattle tattle! Joseph, you are a tattletale!

Zilpah: It's about time to get the mail?

Bilhah: No, Zilpah, it's not time to get the mail. I said, "Joseph, our eldest stepson, is a tattletale!"

(Joseph smirks — acts like he has more to tell)

Zilpah: *(laughs)* And a darn good one, too! *(Joseph and Zilpah laugh together and dance a little jig)*

Bilhah: *(looks sternly)* But they are *our* sons you're talking about, Joseph! They are your brothers! Do you call what you're tattling about good for family unity and respect and good will?

Zilpah: *(more serious)* Yeah, stepson, we only want peace in the family. Blended families need that you know. *Stepson* Joseph are you going to stir up trouble — for your half-brothers?

Joseph: Naw — don't worry. But look what Dad gave me. This beautiful robe with loooooong sleeves.

Bilhah and Zilpah: Wow. That is beautiful! Royal and elegant.

Joseph: It's just like the princes wear. *(shows off and prances around)*

(Bilhah and Zilpah exit. Brothers appear. Joseph continues to parade around. Brothers are talking to themselves — they see Joseph, point to him, make disparaging remarks, some are heard, some are not)

Joseph: Brothers, brothers, brothers, let me tell you a dream I had the other night.

Brothers: A dream? *(groan, mumble, grumble)*

Joseph: *(proceeds nonplussed — dramatically)* There we were all working together. Our family, united and peaceful. Shalom was in the air.

Brothers: *(mock him)* Shalom was in my hair, Shalom was eaten like a pear. Shalom, shalom, shalom.

Joseph: *(blissfully)* We were stacking hay bales on the ranch. You, Reuben. You, Simeon, Levi, and Issachar. You, too, Gad, Asher, and Zebulun. Judah, too. Naphtal and Dan. We worked together like a team. It was beautiful. All of you had stacks of alfalfa hay in my dream. I had the highest stack of all. And you know what?

Reuben: No, what Joe?

Joseph: All of *your* stacks of hay bowed down to *my* stack of hay.

Brothers: Oh, groan. Give us a break. Pretty uppity if you ask us ... Joseph! *(stretch word)*

Joseph: *(leaps up on a box)* And I had another dream. *(Martin Luther King, Jr., style)*

Brothers: *(groan)* Not another one.

Joseph: I dreamed I was an *aeronaut*.

Brothers: Aeronaut?

Joseph: Yes, an aeronaut — a person who flies around the globe in a helium balloon.

Brothers: That's nuts!

Joseph: *(continues)* ... and you my brothers were aeronauts, too. You just had *hot* air balloons — I had a *helium* balloon — the queen of the skies. And you know what?

Brothers: *(fake excitement)* What? What, dearest Joseph? Tell us more.

Joseph: Your hot air balloons dipped and bowed to my helium balloon as I flew around the world — I was the first ever to circumvent the globe!

Brothers: *(grumble)* A prince's robe. Bales of hay bowing down. Balloons bowing down. What a hallucinator!

(Brothers exit. Joseph freezes for the duration of the homily)

(music)

Homily One — Part One
Genesis 37:11
Why Can't We All Just Get Along?

"So his brothers were jealous of him ..." (Genesis 37:11).

My mother once made a lovely woolen sweater for me. It was a work of art. She made it out of colorful woolen strings of yarn. I was amazed by its intricate interwoven patterns that only an artist's eye and nimble fingers could create. I wore it with pride.

One day I noticed a loose string. I pulled on the snag and it got longer and longer and then to my dismay I realized the sweater was unraveling! It was coming apart.

So it is in the story of Joseph and his brothers. The unity, the cohesion of Jacob's family begins to unravel and come apart. Like my sweater with a snag. Pull on it — it's hard to stop. Pull on the yarn long enough and all you end up with is a pile of yarn.

Shalom, the Hebrew word for peace, unity, and good will, like the sweater began to disintegrate. Two snags appear in the story of Joseph and his brothers.

1) The first snag — *favoritism*. Father Jacob gives to Joseph, the son of his favored late wife, Rachel, a coat with long sleeves. The Septuagint Bible calls it a coat of many colors. It is a coat reserved for royalty. A mantle for a prince.

Genesis reports that the brothers saw that their Father Jacob loved Joseph more than any other. You and I know the problem of favoritism in a family.

When one child is elevated above another — that's a recipe for trouble. Sometimes it's only the *perception* of favoritism that is present when mom or dad appears to favor one sibling over another.

All of us have played games with our parents by announcing, "Well, here's your favorite son or daughter."

But favoritism provided the seed for trouble. Then coupled with father Jacob's favoritism, Joseph unwittingly adds fuel to the fire. He brags about two dreams he had in which he appears superior to his brothers. The dreams seem nasty but are in fact prophesies of what is to come — shalom unraveled.

2) The second snag that unravels shalom — is the ten brothers' *jealousy*. "His brothers said to him, 'Are you indeed to reign over us? Are you indeed to have dominion over us?' So they hated him even more ..." (Genesis 37:8).

You and I have known the fire of *jealousy*. We've given it. We've received it! Hot! Burning! Consuming! Scorching and torching relationships.

Jealousy ignites when a family member gets an enriched portion of the inheritance. A fellow employee gets the promotion instead of you. A co-worker gets the raise you expected. Jealousy flames hot in matters of love and romance.

We know where jealousy comes from. Alienation from God and from one another. It comes from our sin. It comes from our low self-esteem, our fears, our insecurities. It comes from an irrational idea that we need to be loved equally by all people all the time or we will be unhappy.

We, too, like the ten brothers, desire the Father's favor. We hunger for favor. We want favor from mom, from dad, from sister, brother, stepdad, or stepmom. We crave family favor, thinking we can wear the sweater of shalom where there is always unity and completeness and total acceptance and unconditional love.

Tonight I hear a cry. In Jacob's family. Also in our families. A lament as the sweater — shalom unravels.

It sounds like the cry we've heard before. Remember the cry of Rodney King? Months after we saw Rodney King's terrible beating over and over and over again on our television screens — later in a court setting Rodney King pleaded, "Why can't we all just get along?"

Why can't we all just get along?

Why?

Now on with our story.

(music)

Scene 2

(Jacob appears on stage. Joseph unfreezes)

Jacob: Joseph, my beloved son.

Joseph: Yes, Dad.

Jacob: Honor the memory of your dear mother, Rachel, and do me a great favor.

Joseph: What is it, Father? You know I would do anything for you.

Jacob: Go and check up on your brothers. They've gone to Shechem, herding my prize flock of sheep. See how they're doing. See if they need any provisions.

Joseph: Yes sir, Father, I will go to Shechem and find my brothers. I'll see how they are doing as you requested. *(exits into the audience and stands)*

(Jacob exits)

Scene 3
(Signbearer walks by with "Shechem" sign)

Joseph: *(to audience)* I am looking for my brothers. This is Shechem, isn't it? *(audience may respond)*

Audience Member: Oh, they went to Dothan. Took a large flock of sheep with them. It's that way. *(points)*

(Traveling music is played by tape or live while Joseph moon-walks like Michael Jackson. Signbearer walks by with "Dothan" sign)

Joseph: Hi, brothers! *(shouts their names as he runs up to them)* Reuben, Simeon, Levi, Issachar, Gad, Asher, Zebulun, Judah, Naphtali, Dan!

(Brothers are stage right. Spot hits them while Joseph is still a ways away)

Brothers: Here comes the dreamer boy. Now what are we in for? *(murmur, complain)* I've got an idea! What is it? Listen up. Let's kill the pain in the neck! *(shake fists, show anger)*

(As Narrator reads Genesis 37:21-36, Brothers and Joseph act out the action as it is read. Bleat like a sheep for a bit of comic relief)

Narrator: But when Reuben heard it, he delivered him out of their hands, saying, "Let us not take his life." Reuben said to them, "Shed no blood; throw him into this pit here in the wilderness, but lay no hand on him" — that he might rescue him out of their hands and restore him to his father.

So when Joseph came to his brothers, they stripped him of his robe, the long robe with sleeves that he wore; and they took him and threw him into a pit. The pit was empty; there was no water in it. Then they sat down to eat; and looking up they saw a caravan of Ishmaelites coming from Gilead, with their camels carrying gum, balm, and resin, on their way to carry it down to Egypt.

Then Judah said to his brothers, "What profit is it if we kill our brother and conceal his blood? Come, let us sell him to the Ishmaelites, and not lay our hands on him, for he is our brother, our own flesh."

And the brothers agreed. When some Midianite traders passed by, they drew Joseph up, lifting him out of the pit, and sold him to the Ishmaelites for twenty pieces of silver. And the Ishmaelites took Joseph to Egypt.

When Reuben returned to the pit and saw that Joseph was not in the pit, he tore his clothes. He returned to his brothers, and said, "The boy is gone; and I, where can I turn?"

Then they took Joseph's robe, slaughtered a goat, and dipped the robe in the blood. They had the long robe with sleeves taken to their father, and they said, "This we have found; see now whether it is your son's robe or not."

The father recognized it and said, "It is my son's robe! A wild animal has devoured him; Joseph is, without doubt, torn to pieces." Then Jacob tore his garments, and put sackcloth on his loins, and mourned for his son many days. All his sons and his daughters sought to comfort him; but he refused to be comforted, and said, "No. I shall go down to Sheol to my son, mourning." Thus his father bewailed him.

Meanwhile, the Midianites had sold him in Egypt to Potiphar, one of Pharaoh's officials, the captain of the guard.

Homily One — Part Two
Genesis 37:35
Why Can't We All Just Get Along?

"All his sons and daughters sought to comfort him; but he refused to be comforted, and said, 'No I shall go down to Sheol to my son, mourning' " (Genesis 37:35).

Aleichem shalom. *(Peace be unto you.)*

Aleichem shalom is both a greeting and a description of right relationships. Aleichem shalom is a desire that you and I have healthy relationships with our family with God and with the entire created order.

23

We are seeing the sweater of peace and unity unravel and unravel. Shalom, that fragile clay jar, is dropped. It shatters! Jacob's family is riddled with *favoritism*, *sibling rivalry*, and *jealousy*. It reeks with *hatred*. The story, at this point, ends with Jacob in deep mourning for the loss of his favorite son, Joseph, and for the loss of shalom in his family. There is no peace, no wholesome unity nor love.

But the good news tonight is that Christ is the key to peace in any family. If your family is in strife, broken, and alienated — start with Jesus Christ.

We read in Ephesians 2:13: "But now in Christ Jesus you who once were far off have been brought near by the blood of Christ. For he is our Peace — in his flesh he has made both groups into one."

You and I have been brought together by Jesus.

The advice columnists are kept busy these days. A letter came to a columnist: "Help: My sister and her husband and children ..." and it went on to pour out a litany of disgust over who in the family got a certain gift and who didn't.

There are multiple examples of peaceless families, wordless "Shalom Aleichems."

Tonight on this Ash Wednesday we experience shalom. Aleichem shalom to the nth degree.

Youth and family come together in unity and love at this most holy place — at the Lord's Table. Around the table we are one. One with God and one with one another.

Come believing that Jesus is your peace. Come trusting that in the bread and wine you receive Jesus. Your sins are covered. Your peace is secured. Your relationships mended.

No longer do we need to lament, "Why can't we all just get along?"

Shalom at last is ours.

(music)

Hey Joe
(Joseph's Rise And Fall)
Genesis 39:1-23

Charactors
> Narrator
> Joseph (good looking)
> Potiphar
> Potiphar's Wife (beautiful, seductress, sleazy)
> Servants (nonspeaking)
> Signbearer (nonspeaking)

Props
> Couch, furniture, large water pitcher, vase, plants (can be real or plastic), "Applause" sign, "Boo" sign, "Frown" sign, "Groan" sign

Setting
> Potiphar's house

(music intro)

Narrator: After Joseph was sold to the traveling Ishmaelites, he was brought to the great nation — Egypt. There in Egypt he was sold as a slave to an officer of the Pharaoh by the name of Potiphar! Potiphar was the captain of Pharaoh's guard — a man of respect and power. Now this officer, Potiphar, had a wife — Ooh La La — what a wife! You'll hear about her in just a minute.

But now let's look in and see how Joseph is doing in this strange land, strange customs, strange language, strange everything. Oh, Joseph, there — how are you doing?

Joseph: I've often asked myself as of late — oh what is happening to me? For all that my brothers did to me and here I am in this

25

place called Egypt. I'm a slave, would you believe it? Sold by my own flesh and blood brothers. Here I am a Hebrew in this Egyptian culture. Their ways are odd. Their language is Greek — oops — I mean Egyptian. But God is with me, I know. I'll have to make the best of it.

Narrator: Joseph did very well! In every responsibility he accepted, he excelled. Everything he touched became a success. His master Potiphar saw that the Lord was with Joseph and was impressed.

(Potiphar enters)

Potiphar: Hey, Servant Joseph! I must speak with you.

Joseph: Yes Sir, Master Potiphar. *(bows)*

Potiphar: I have noticed that you are doing excellent work in my household.

Joesph: Thank you, Sir. Thank you very much.

Potiphar: I have been thinking and in light of your performance I am going to promote you to chief of my household.

Joseph: Oh, Sir, that would truly be an honor. I will do my very best.

Potiphar: I am appointing you overseer of my entire estate. From now on you are in charge. *(drum roll optional)*

Joseph: Thank you, Sir, thank you, your esteemed one. I shall honor your trust. I shall keep the trust you have in me.

(music)

Homily Two — Part One
Genesis 39:6
Trust And Faith

"So he left all that he had in Joseph's charge and, with him there, he had no concern for anything but the food that he ate" (Genesis 39:6).

It is a great thing to be able to trust someone. The rock foundation of marriage is trust. Healthy families thrive on trust. Public officials get elected if they can prove they are trustworthy. The center and core of faith is based on trust.

When trust is broken, violated, mutilated, rejected, scorned, or lost, relationships go sour and become hollow. Trust is the glue for healthy living.

After working for years inventing a light bulb, Thomas Edison finally succeeded. He was happy, to say the least. As Michael Guido tells it in *Seeds From The Sower*, handing the first light bulb to his lab boy, Edison said, "Take it downstairs and we will turn it on." Nervous with excitment, the lab assistant tripped and fell, breaking the precious bulb. So Thomas Edison went on to make the second bulb. When finished — what did he do? He trusted the same young man and said, "Take it downstairs and we will turn it on."

Potiphar, the chief of Pharaoh's guard gave Joseph his complete trust. "You're in charge, Joseph, I trust you."

Trust begins in little things. "He who is faithful," Jesus said, "in very little is faithful also in much; and he who is dishonest in very little, is dishonest also in much. If then you have not been faithful in money, who will entrust to you the true riches?" It's the little things — even trifling things that can make a big, big difference.

In 1920, King Alexander of Greece, a peace-loving ruler, was bitten by his pet monkey. He developed blood poisoning and died. A general election led to the recall of King Constantine who unfortunately ignited a disastrous war with the Turks. The slaughter was staggering. Winston Churchill reflecting on the incident years later said, "A quarter of a million persons died because of that monkey's bite."

27

Did you know that eminent scientist Charles Darwin's last great research was done on a simple little *earthworm*?

George Herbert, Shakespeare's contemporary wrote: "For want of a nail, the shoe is lost; for want of a shoe, the horse is lost; for want of a horse, the rider is lost...."

Little things can matter a great deal. A monkey bite, an earthworm, a nail. The one who is trusted in very little is trusted also in much.

Potiphar's trust in Joseph started with little things, then went to bigger and bigger things.

Trust. In whom do you and I trust?

We are fortunate. Our next door neighbor Ken, is our Joseph. When we go away for a few days, we give Ken the key and say, "Watch our house, let in the plumber, and feed the cats." It's wonderful to trust people, parents, children, neighbors, and coworkers. But its even greater to trust the message on a nickel. What's on a nickel but, "In God We Trust." The same message as Proverbs 3:5: "Trust in the Lord with all your heart and do not rely on your own insight."

Ever wondered how this message of trust got on this nickel?

In the dark days of the Civil War, a country pastor, who was also a farmer, wrote to Secretary of the Treasury Salmon P. Chase, asking that some suitable recognition of God be placed upon our coinage. He suggested the words "God, Liberty, Law." Secretary Chase was in sympathy with the idea but Congress objected until finally on April 22, 1864, Congress authorized a two-cent piece upon which was stamped the motto, "In God We Trust" (Source Unknown).

Isaiah said it and the people sang it, "Surely God is my salvation, I will trust and not be afraid for the Lord God is my strength and my might; he has become my salvation" (Isaiah 12:2).

Trust is not easy.

Remember the climber story? A climber fell off a cliff. As he tumbled down in the huge canyon, he grabbed hold of a branch of a small tree. "Help!" he shouted. "Is there anybody up there?" A deep majestic voice from the sky echoed through the canyon. "I

will help you my son. But first you must have faith and trust me."
"All right, all right, I trust you," answered the climber. The voice
replied, "First let go of the branch." There was a long pause and
the climber shouted again, "Is there anyone else up there?" Not so
with Joseph — he trusted God as Potiphar trusted him. Now on to
our story ...

(music — melodrama style)

Narrator: Everything was going fine. The trust Potiphar had in
Joseph was amazing. But now, my friends, listen to a melodrama.
A melodrama like you're never heard before from Holy Writ. It
has suspense, intrigue, romance of sorts, a villainess, a judge, and
not necessarily a happy ending at least for the present.

Meet our hero. *(Joseph takes a bow. [melodrama music] Signbearer shows "Applause" sign)*

Meet our villainess. *(Potiphar's wife takes a bow. [music] Signbearer displays "Boo" sign)*

Meet our judge. *(Mr. Potiphar takes a bow. [music] Signbearer
displays "Frown")*

The problem began when Joseph — tall and handsome —
(Joseph beams) succeeded in running Potiphar's entire household.
And in Potiphar's house is Potiphar's wife! *(Mrs. Potiphar smiles
seductively as she dances around, bows, prances, and then sits in
the corner of stage right watching Joseph do certain household
duties. Mrs. Potiphar whispers in Joseph's ear. He recoils looking
horrified! He busies himself. Mrs. Potiphar takes her cloak and
throws it over him — he reacts and rejects her — gets super busy
with work to avoid her. She chases him. They run through the
sanctuary)*

Narrator: Mrs. Potiphar would not give up. Every time Joseph
came around she would say:

Potiphar's Wife: Hey, Joe, hey, Joey Joe. *(romantic music; they
freeze)*

Narrator: One day when Joseph was doing his household chores *(Joseph unfreezes and waters plants)* along came Mrs. Potiphar —

Potiphar's Wife: Hey, Joseph *(in a melodic voice),* it's time to pay the rent!

Joseph: Huh? Oh no, no! *(Flees)*

(She grabs his cloak — he runs away. She is stunned [music] then angered — then puts on evil eyes)

Potiphar's Wife: *(screams, feigns rejection, and lies)* See what my husband did! Brought this filthy Hebrew into *my* house! He wanted to have an affair with me! *(dramatically)* I screamed at such a revolting, frightening experience and he ran away thank goodness!

(Servants run in and out frantically and are aghast at the accusation)

Narrator: When Potiphar the master heard the charges of his devoted wife he blew his stack. Enraged he took Joseph and sent him to jail!

(Potiphar escorts Joseph off to jail)

Narrator: In most melodramas, the hero and the victim win. Our melodrama is not ended. Our hero is still in jail. *(Signbearer walks by with "Groan" sign)* Mrs. Potiphar — our villain *("Boo" sign)* isn't caught for her temptress ways, her lies, her deceit. *("Boo" sign)* In fact we don't hear about her again. Will justice be served?

(music; Signbearer displays "Applause" sign)

Homily Two — Part Two
Genesis 39:21
WWJD?

"But the Lord was with Joseph and showed him his steadfast love...."

WWJD? That's the question tonight. Some of you young people may be wearing or have seen the bracelet with the letters WWJD woven into it. They're a hot selling item these days. The latest mail-order advertisement that I have seen is also selling the question on coffee mugs, ball caps, back packs, and Bible covers. WWJD?

Our story from Joseph tonight asks the WWJD question, "What would *Joseph* do?" It was clear what Joseph did. He resisted the ploy and the temptation of Potiphar's wife. She and her ruby lips wanted a steamy relationship with this handsome young man. But Joseph said, "No." He would not violate his master's trust. He would not break shalom. What would Joseph do? He would maintain his sterling character and God-fearing morality.

The WWJD cloth bracelets began as a fundraiser by a group of Grand Rapids kids who were trying to raise money for service projects — but the bracelets caught on. They became so popular that sales topped $1 million and they continue to sell.

When you and I are tempted, it's a good question to ask — WWJD? But we can go further with the original intent — WWJD? What would *Jesus* do? Wear your disciple bracelet on your wrist or on your heart and know that as disciples of Christ we love and we live according to God's grace and God's calling which sets us apart from the rest of the world.

Help us, O God, by your power to resist the devil and stand with Joseph and you our Lord Jesus. Amen.

(music)

Dreams Come True

Genesis 40-41:57

Characters
>Narrator
>Photographer
>Joseph
>Cupbearer
>Baker
>Pharaoh
>Servants (nonspeaking)
>Signbearer (nonspeaking)

Props
>Old-time camera with hood and a working flash, prison bars, Joseph's Granary (diagram on page 102), special hat, signs: "Ooo," "Wow," "Great Idea!" "Applause," "Groan"

Setting
>Joseph is behind bars. With him is the Cupbearer and the Baker. (Cupbearer and Baker may be dressed in modern clothes that convey their individual professions)

Notes
>Timing is important with appropriate "spaces" in the reading and acting. Not *all* the narrative needs to be acted out. Actors may simply deliberately and visually "freeze" at times. Photographer may inject a little comic relief by his/her antics.

(music)

Scene 1

(Narrator is at podium; Joseph, Cupbearer, and Baker are in prison)

Narrator: Some time after this, the cupbearer of the king of Egypt and his baker offended their lord the king of Egypt. Pharaoh was angry with his two officers, the chief cupbearer and the chief baker, and he put them in custody in the house of the captain of the guard, in the prison where Joseph was confined (Genesis 40:1-3). *(points to where Joseph, Cupbearer, and Baker are imprisoned)*

(music from the '20s or '30s)

(Photographer methodically takes a picture of each of the prisoners, one at a time in three individual settings outside of the prison bars with three individual "flashes"; music ends)

Narrator: The captain of the guard charged Joseph with them, and he waited on them; and they continued for some time in custody. One night they both dreamed — the cupbearer and the baker of the king of Egypt, who were confined in the prison — each his own dream, and each dream with its own meaning. When Joseph came to them in the morning, he saw that they were troubled. So he asked Pharaoh's officers, who were with him in custody in his master's house, "Why are your faces downcast today?" They said to him, "We have had dreams, and there is no one to interpret them." And Joseph said to them, "Do not interpretations belong to God? Please tell them to me" (Genesis 40:4-8). *(pause)*

Narrator: So the chief cupbearer told his dream to Joseph, and said to him, "In my dream there was a vine before me, and on the vine there were three branches. As soon as it budded, its blossoms came out and the clusters ripened into grapes. Pharaoh's cup was in my hand; and I took the grapes and pressed them into Pharaoh's cup, and placed the cup in Pharaoh's hand." Then Joseph said to him, "This is its interpretation: the three branches are three days; within three days Pharaoh will lift up your head and restore you to your office; and you shall place Pharaoh's cup in his hand, just as you used to do when you were his cupbearer. But remember me when it is well with you; please do me the kindness to make mention of me to Pharaoh, and so get me out of this place. For in fact I was stolen out of the land of the Hebrews; and here also I have done nothing that they should have put me into the dungeon" (Genesis 40:9-15). *(Cupbearer holds his dream with an outstretched hand as if it is a tangible thing. Photographer focuses on the "dream" in the Cupbearer's hand and takes a picture)*

Narrator: When the chief baker saw that the interpretation was favorable, he said to Joseph, "I also had a dream: there were three cake baskets on my head, and in the uppermost basket there were all sorts of baked food for Pharaoh, but the birds were eating it out of the basket on my head." And Joseph answered, "This is its interpretation: the three baskets are three days; within three days Pharaoh will lift up your head — from you! — and hang you on a pole; and the birds will eat the flesh from you" (40:16-19). *(Baker holds his dream in his outstretched hand as if it is also a tangible thing while Photographer takes a picture of it)*

Narrator: On the third day, which was Pharaoh's birthday, he made a feast for all his servants, and lifted up the head of the chief cupbearer and the head of the chief baker among his servants. He restored the chief cupbearer to his cupbearing, and he placed the cup in Pharaoh's hand; but the chief baker he hanged, just as Joseph had interpreted to them. Yet the chief cupbearer did not remember Joseph, but forgot him (Genesis 40:20-23).

(musical interlude)

(Cupbearer, Servants, and Pharaoh enter. Photographer takes a poised picture of Pharaoh. Pharaoh then acts out the drama of the text while Narrator describes his dream)

Narrator: After two whole years, Pharaoh dreamed that he was standing by the Nile, and there came up out of the Nile seven sleek and fat cows, and they grazed in the reed grass. Then seven other

35

cows, ugly and thin, came up out of the Nile after them, and stood by the other cows on the bank of the Nile. The ugly and thin cows ate up the seven sleek and fat cows. And Pharaoh awoke. Then he fell asleep and dreamed a second time; seven ears of grain, plump and good, were growing on one stalk. Then seven ears, thin and blighted up by the east wind, sprouted after them. The thin ears swallowed up the seven plump and full ears. Pharaoh awoke, and it was a dream. In the morning his spirit was troubled; so he sent and called for the magicians of Egypt and all its wise men. Pharaoh told them his dreams, but there was no one who could interpret them to Pharaoh (Genesis 41:1-8).

Cupbearer: Oh my, I remember my faults today! I forgot, I forgot, I forgot! There is *one* who can interpret your dreams, O most high Pharaoh.

Pharaoh: Out with it! Who is it?

Cupbearer: Once Pharaoh was angry with his servants *(bows down),* and put me and the chief baker in custody in the house of the captain of the guard. We dreamed on the same night, he and I, and each having a dream with its own meaning. A young Hebrew was there with us, a servant of the captain of the guard (Genesis 41:10-12a).

Pharaoh: Go on, go on!

Cupbearer: When we told him, he interpreted our dreams to us, giving an interpretation to each according to his dream. As he interpreted to us, so it turned out: I was restored to my office (Genesis 12b-13). *(Signbearer shows "Applause" sign)* And the baker was hanged. *(Signbearer shows "Groan" sign)*

Pharaoh: Send for that young Hebrew at once! *(all freeze)*

Narrator: Then Pharaoh sent for Joseph, and he was hurriedly brought out of the dungeon. When he had shaved himself and changed his clothes, he came in before Pharaoh (Genesis 41:14). *(Joseph enters; all unfreeze)*

Pharaoh: I have had a dream that none of these numskulls *(points toward nonpresent court jesters)* can seem to interpret. Can *you* interpret this most troublesome dream? *(whispers in Joseph's ear)*

Joseph: Possibly. Though it is not I. It is God who will give Pharaoh a favorable answer. Your dreams, your highness, of seven cows and seven ears of grain are one and the same.

Pharaoh: Oh really?

Photographer: *(Aside)* Oh reilly! *(gives "O here we go again" look)*

Joseph: Yes, O Pharaoh, majestic ruler of all Egypt. The seven good cows and seven good ears of grain are seven years of good crops and good food. The seven bad cows and bad ears of grain are seven terrible years of famine coming on the land. If you are wise you'll get ready for what's coming. *(actors freeze)*

(music)

Homily Three — Part One
Genesis 41:15, 16
God's Dream For You

And Pharaoh said to Joseph, "I have had a dream, and there is no one who can interpret it. I have heard it said of you that when you hear a dream you can interpret it." Joseph answered Pharaoh, "It is not I: God will give Pharaoh a favorable answer" (Genesis 41:15, 16).

Friends in Christ, a common experience for all of us is to dream. Night dreams. Day dreams. Dreams of delight. Dreams of despair. Dreams about beauty and love. Dreams so dark and dreadful we call them nightmares. Dreams vague, misty, and mysterious. Dreams so real they merge with reality.

Once I dreamed I was running through the meadows and suddenly came upon a snake in the grass. It was so real I recoiled and actually fell out of bed on the bedroom floor. My wife cried out anxiously, "What is it now?" I told her. We both laughed.

From the book of Genesis through the book of Revelation, dreams and visions were regarded as one way, a most important way that God spoke to humankind.

In the Hebrew language there is no clear distinction between dreams and visions. They were seen as different aspects of the same reality — the world beyond sense experience. The Hebrew word for dream, *chalom*, means to be strong and healthy. Dream experiences were often referred to as "visions of the night" as in Job 21:8; Isaiah 29:7; and Daniel 7:2.

The book of Daniel is full of dreams and dream interpretations. When Daniel and the king converse, Daniel's response to the king's question as to why he dreams, has given us the essentials of modern dream theory. Daniel speaks, "The dream has come to you O King, in order that you may know the thoughts of your inmost mind" (Daniel 2:28).

How often dreams express anxieties, insecurities, hopes, and longings in one's subconscious.

The New Testament also considers dreams as a means of direct communication from God to people. Remember how dreams directed and determined the life of Joseph, Mary, and the baby Jesus? In a little more than a chapter of the Gospel of Matthew (1:18—2:23) dreams influence the course of Jesus' life four times and a fifth dream revelation affects the wise men who brought the baby Jesus gifts.

We see *three* significant dream sequences in the story of Joseph.
1. Joseph's dreams of himself and his brothers.
2. The baker's and the cupbearer's dreams in prison.
3. The Pharaoh's dream of a mysterious future.

The significance for us is to recall the fulfillment of God in every biblical dream and then to think carefully about our present dreams and visions.

First pay attention to your *night dreams*. They are filled with unexpressed emotions and various feelings. All rooted in thought and experience. Night dreams usually have meanings.

The late Swiss psychologist, C. G. Jung, saw the dream as a guide to the soul. "Night dreams," he said, "brought an offering of healing to people because it compensated for our limited consciousness and egocentricity by bringing us closer to our inner center."

Secondly, pay attention to your daytime visions. The New Testament word *noema* refers to vision. A day vision is to be able to see something in the future and then be a part of its coming to fruition.

The prophet Habakkuk (2:3) said, "For the vision still has its time, presses on to fulfillment and will not disappoint. If it delays wait for it — it will surely come."

In our personal and institutional life, lack of vision seems to be more prevalent than the presence and power of vision. Here are some examples:

They said of one man. Can't act. Slightly bald. Can dance a little. That was the text of the memo written in 1933 by an MGM testing/casting director. The memo described an aspiring entertainer who didn't make the grade. His name was Fred Astaire.

A so-called expert once said of football coach Vince Lombardi, "He possesses minimal football knowledge. Lacks motivation."

The teachers of Ludwig von Beethoven called him hopeless as a composer. Beethoven handled the violin awkwardly and wouldn't work at improving his technique.

Of Enrico Caruso, the great opera singer, they once said, "He had no voice at all and could not sing."

Author Louisa May Alcott who wrote the classic, *Little Women*, was advised by her family to find work as a servant or seamstress.

Walt Disney was once fired by a newspaper for lacking ideas.

Jesus was crucified for his outspoken understanding of God.

The famous Thomas Watson, chairman of IBM said in 1943: "I think there is a world market for maybe five computers." Even Bill Gates, the great visionary, postulated in 1981 that 640K ought to be enough for anybody.

As Joseph dreamed and paid attention to the dreams of others, so it is opportune for you and me to, "Pay attention to our night dreams and our day visions."

Especially, we need to allow our day visions to work for God and hasten the coming of the kingdom.

Pastor Dick Meyer tells, "A woman came into my office the other day. As we talked, she relayed a wonderful story. Her former congregation had very few children. One day she set up a table in the church's fellowship hall. She placed children's curriculum on the table. Someone asked her the purpose for the table. She said, 'That's for our fifth and sixth grade class.' That same person said, 'We don't have enough children for a fifth and sixth grade class.' She replied, 'We will soon.' "

That's the vision expected of God's people.

May God give you the ability to dream dreams and see visions of what God has in store.

Joseph said it accurately, "It is not I: it is God who will give Pharaoh a favorable answer."

Now back to Joseph.

(music)

Scene 2

Narrator: After Joseph had interpreted Pharaoh's dream of seven cows — fat and marbled, grazing in lush green grass and *suddenly* eaten by seven lean and hungry cows and seven ears of grain being eaten by seven thin and blighted ears of grain as seven years of plenty and then seven years of famine — Joseph gave this sound advice:

Joseph: Your Highness — Pharaoh of all Egypt *(bows)* — I humbly suggest that you find a gifted person who is discerning and wise to give leadership in your department of agriculture.

Pharaoh: *(angrily)* You mean I'm not capable to lead my country Egypt in a time of crisis?

Joseph: Oh, no Sir, I mean oh, yes Sir, I mean, I mean ...

Pharaoh: Well, what do you mean? Spit it out! Time's awasting!

Joseph: Oh, Sir — you are most capable, most wise, most discerning but this is a special circumstance. This is an extraordinary situation with unusual needs.

Pharaoh: *(calmed down)* Okay. How then should this discerning, wise, and gifted "subordinate to me" leader lead? What do you propose Hebrew?

Joseph: Well, Sir, I humbly *(bows)* suggest you appoint overseers of the land. Set up a national grain reserve in the cities as a hedge against the coming famine. When the seven years of famine do come you will be ready. And the world will applaud you.

(Signbearer shows signs to audience — "Ooo," "Wow," "Great Idea!" and "Applause")

Pharaoh: We've answered "What?" Now the question is "Who?" In whom can I find the Spirit of God? One who is wise and discerning and sensible for this country? *(Goes out and ad libs, asking the audience — he keeps asking until someone suggests "Joseph." Joseph smiles and nods)* Hey — you — Joseph — the Hebrew man from Canaan — you shall be the one! Since your God has shown you all this — obviously there is no one so discerning and wise as *you*! *(Places a special hat on Joseph's head)*

Joseph: *(bows)* Thank you, your eminence.

(Photographer takes picture of Joseph with his new regal hat on)

Narrator: So Joseph became an overseer and guided the collection of food during the years of plenty. We call it "Joseph's Granary." *(points to Granary where food has been collected for the local food shelves)*

(music)

Homily Three — Part Two
Genesis 41:57
Joseph The Provider

"Moreover all the world came to Joseph in Egypt to buy grain, because the famine became severe throughout the world" (Genesis 41:57).

I am holding a loaf of bread in my hand. If you took it to the mall parking lot you could hardly give it away. If you took this loaf of bread to Egypt today many families would scramble to get it. But take it to places in Africa, Haiti, or India where millions are starving you would have a small riot for want of it.

Joseph became the benevolent provider for the then-known world. His pantry was full. His granary accessible to all. His planning and foresight benefited the hungry.

Today Joseph's granary is needed again. Hunger of a chronic nature affects 500 million to 1 billion people around the world. One out of every eight people in the world suffers from hunger.

Undernutrition and malnutrition lead to the deaths of 40,000 children a day — that's approximately fifteen million a year.

Crop failures, floods, and other natural disasters contribute to hunger, but they are not the root causes. There is enough food to eat in the world but people cannot afford to buy it. War, distribution problems, the powerful and rich refusing to share, and our indulgent food and resource wasting lifestyle are big problems. Ultimately poverty itself is the root cause.

Hunger and malnutrition not only kill, but leave physical defects. Each year 250,000 people, mostly children, go blind due to vitamin deficiency. There are 32 million poor Americans in the United States. Children account for thirteen million of the poor.

Joseph is busy today, too — Joseph and his helpers. You and I are the hands of Joseph, the heart of Jesus, and the compassion central to the mission of the Body of Christ.

So we join hands with food pantries, blanket makers, Lutheran World Relief, Church World Service, Heifer Project International,

Catholic Relief Service, Mennonite Central Committee, World Vision, and Habitat for Humanity in order to care for the poor and feed the hungry of the world.

Thank you, God, for Joseph's granaries. Thank you, God, for hearts full of wisdom, discernment, and the sacrificial love of Christ. Amen.

Optional: Let us sing, "We Need Bread For The World" (found on page 12).

The Brothers Meet
(Brotherhood Or Brothers Of The Hood?)
Genesis 42 & 43

Characters
> Reader
> Narrator (may be the same person as Reader)
> Aide
> Guard
> Joseph
> Ten Brothers
> Benjamin
> Court Jester (nonspeaking)
> Signbearer (nonspeaking)

Props
> Ten Brothers are dressed in Palestinian costumes except all wear cowboy hats and Lone Ranger type black masks, sign that reads "3 Days Pass," banquet table and chairs

Setting
> The scene opens in Joseph's palatial office

(music)

Scene 1
Reader: When Jacob learned that there was grain in Egypt, he said to his sons, "Why do you keep looking at one another? I have heard," he said, "that there is grain in Egypt; go down and buy grain for us there, that we may live and not die." So ten of Joseph's brothers went down to buy grain in Egypt. But Jacob did not send Joseph's brother Benjamin with his brothers, for he feared that harm might come to him. Thus the sons of Israel were among the other people who came to buy grain, for the famine had reached the land of Canaan (Genesis 42:1-5).

45

Aide: *(pompously)* Hear ye, hear ye — honorable Joseph — administrator par excellence over the entire land of Egypt — all powerful, all supreme, except for our eminence the Pharaoh. Most excellent, wise, discerning *(looks at audience)*, good-looking, and handsome *(Guard swats him into reality)*, oh, yes, aah ...

Guard: Get to the point! *(threatens with spear)*

Aide: Okay, okay ... announcing visitors from the northeast — ten visitors and their servants from Canaan who wish to buy grain in this time of greaaaaaaaat famine. Presentingggg the brothers ten from Canaan. *(music or drum roll option)*

Joseph: *(motions to enter)* Oh yes, thank you. Please show them in.

Aide: Pronto.

Joseph: Hmmmm, let's see what they want.

(Ten Brothers enter and bow down to the floor)

Joseph: *(to the audience as an aside)* Oh my goodness! Look who is here! All ten of my delinquent brothers. Let's see. Reuben, Simeon, Levi, Judah, Issachar, Zebulun, hmm, Dan and Naphtali, aah, Gad and Asher, hmmm no Benjamin. I see they don't recognize me. My perverse side of me says, "It is good to see them again after all these years. I wonder if they're as crooked and deceitful as they've always been." *(to the Brothers, sternly)* Get up! Hebrews! What is it you want? Speak up!

Reuben: *(Brothers get up to their knees)* Oh, Sir, your eminence. We are hungry.

Brothers: *(ad lib)* Oh yes, we are hungry. Hungry. Hungry. We are without food. Can you help sir from your abundant granaries?

Reuben: We are from the land of Canaan. Our father Jacob sent us to ...

Joseph: *(stands up excitedly)* You have a father who is *alive*?

Reuben: Oh yes, Sir. Our esteemed father Jacob sent us to get some ...

Joseph: *(harshly)* Where did you say you came from?

Reuben: Canaan ...

Joseph: You are spies! Spies! You have come to see the nakedness of the land!

Judah: No, no, Sir. *(bows and bows and bows)* We have come to buy food.

Aide: *(butts in with incongruent behavior in a mocking high pitched voice)* You've come to be rude to our excellency! Well, I'm the honorable overseer's exercise guru. You're in the mood to be rude, eh?

Brothers: *(look at each other, confused)* Wha...

Aide: To the mats! *(Brothers all plop down on their bellies)* Exercise time. Okay ten push ups. Hey, hey one and a two and a three.... Now some leg lifts. On your backs! Up, up, up.

Joseph: Oh stop it — they are only spies! Not in the mood to be rude. Guards, guards to prison for these spies!

(Brothers meekly exit to prison)

(musical interlude)

(Signbearer walks by with "3 Days Pass" sign)

Aide: Your excellency! The brothers ten from Canaan! *(Brothers enter)*

Joseph: How was your stay in prison? Hospitable, I hope.

Brothers: *(feigned happiness)* Oh, yes, the accommodations were lovely. Good food, good hard floor ... as good as any Marriott ... good guards ... friendly rats ...

Joseph: All right, all right. Maybe you are *not* spies intending to sniff out the nakedness of the land here in Egypt — I will take a chance on you. I'll sell you some grain. What do you need? I have plenty. *(moves out of sight of the Brothers and weeps)* Oh this is amazing! My brothers, my brothers, right here in Egypt!

Guard: *(picks up sacks of grain from Joseph's granary and gives it to the Brothers)* Here you are Canaanites, as you desired.

(Joseph returns)

Joseph: You may depart to your home in Canaan but to be sure I am going to keep one of you as collateral! *(Brothers look dismayed)* You! *(points to Simeon)* Tie him up! He'll be my ace in the hole.

Brothers: *(in a repentant mood)* Oh what did we do to deserve this? We've always been decent law-abiding citizens haven't we? What's going to happen to us now?

Brother: No — we haven't always been decent, loyal brothers — what did we do to our long lost brother Joseph? That was inexcusable. *(Brothers nod agreement one by one as they take off their "Lone Ranger" masks and hats and look sheepishly repentant)*

Brother: What fools! We saw our brother Joseph's anguish but we didn't listen. Now we're going to lose Simeon. If only we could undo what we have done.

A Brother: Well, it's time to go back to our father Jacob. Dad's waiting. Bye, Simeon. *(hugs him)* We'll be back.

(Brothers exit)

(music)

Homily Four — Part One
Genesis 42:21
The Brothers' Conversion

They said to one another, "Alas, we are paying the penalty for what we did to our brother; we saw his anguish when he pleaded with us, but we would not listen" (Genesis 42:21).

I want to say today, a good word for guilt. You heard me rightly. Guilt. Plain old-fashioned guilt. Not pseudo-guilt. Not pathological guilt. And surely not shame. The difference between guilt and shame is that guilt says "I did something wrong" whereas shame says "I am no good." That, of course, is a lie.

The brothers ten were smitten! They were struck by pure, unadulterated guilt! They had done something very bad in the past. The dark deeds they had done to Joseph had never been uncovered, acknowledged, confessed, nor resolved. Covered lies get moldy. Awful deeds stink like rotten cabbage in your refrigerator.

Guilt overshadowed the brothers ten as they stood in Joseph's very presence that day — even though they didn't know him.

Joseph continues to be hard. No quick or cheap forgiveness. Repentance must be real. A true conversion insists that the brothers stop and look at past deeds that now set their guilt in motion.

Lately, I've been hearing only bad words about guilt. It's as though the enemy of a happy, carefree life is to dismiss and dispense with guilt as quickly as possible. I regularly hear comments like: "Don't lay a guilt trip on me." "Stop trying to make me feel guilty." "Guilt isn't a good motivation for change."

Contrast this with an article I received in the mail recently titled, "In Praise of Guilt." It quoted Dr. Willard Gaylin, clinical professor of psychiatry at Columbia University's College of Physicians and Surgeons. Dr. Gaylin notes that inappropriate guilt, like other inappropriate emotions, is destructive, but that does not make guilt bad. Good guilt is not guilty fear. Guilty fear is fear of punishment for wrongdoing. We feel guilty fear when we become afraid of being caught violating external standards. Good guilt, on the other hand recognizes the failure to live up to internal standards. Good guilt is an emotion of maturity. It presupposes internalized standards. Good guilt blossoms in an alive and developed *conscience*.

The Bible speaks of people who have a weak conscience (1 Corinthians 8:7), a defiled conscience (Titus 1:15), and a seared conscience (1 Timothy 4:2). A healthy conscience is a gift.

There is a story of a prince who received a ring from a renowned magician. It was a beautiful ring set with diamonds and rubies and pearls. "Great Master," said the magician, "that which I have given you has more value then the beautiful gems incrusted into it. It has a rare and mystic property which you will soon discover." The prince found that the ring rested easily enough on his finger in ordinary circumstances, but as soon as he formed a bad thought, or committed an evil action, the ring became a monitor. It would contract immediately and painfully on his finger, warning him of sin lurking at the door.

The legend carries a powerful truth.

The poorest of us possess this valuable jewel. The ring of the fable is like the voice of God in our conscience. Our conscience is a valuable asset, though it is not infallible.

The ten brothers' consciences began to work. The Holy Spirit began the work of transformation. We saw the brothers in the dramily take off their hats and remove their masks as an outward sign of an inward change. The Holy Spirit clears away guilt and pronounces forgiveness in the name of Christ.

The good news that is ours tonight is that in Christ there is forgiveness. "If we confess our sins, God is faithful and just and will forgive us our sins and cleanse us from all unrighteousness" (1 John 1:9).

Good guilt is good. It serves a positive function. It highlights our sins and weaknesses — our need of God's grace both to forgive and to empower us to break out of our bad patterns of living.

God grant you good guilt and beyond that full forgiveness and the power to forgive others.

Amen.

(music)

Scene 2

(at Joseph's banquet table)

Reader: In Canaan, as they were emptying their sacks they found that in each one's sack was his bag of money. When they and their father saw their bundles of money, they were dismayed. Their father Jacob said to them, "I am the one you have bereaved of children: Joseph is no more, and Simeon is no more, and now you would take Benjamin. All this has happened to me!" Then Reuben said to his father, "You may kill my two sons if I do not bring him back to you. Put him in my hands, and I will bring him back to you." But he said, "My son shall not go down with you, for his brother is dead, and he alone is left. If harm should come to him on the journey that you are to make, you would bring down my gray hairs with sorrow to Sheol."

Now the famine was severe in the land. And when they had eaten up the grain that they had brought from Egypt, their father said to them, "Go again, buy us a little more food." But Judah said to him, "The man solemnly warned us, saying, 'You shall not see my face unless your brother is with you.' If you will send our brother with us, we will go down and buy you food; but if you will not send him, we will not go down for the man said to us, 'You shall not see my face, unless your brother is with you.' Israel said, "Why did you treat me so badly as to tell the man that you had another brother?" They replied, "The man questioned us carefully about ourselves and our kindred, saying, 'Is your father still alive?

51

Have you another brother?' What we told him was in answer to these questions. Could we in any way know that he would say, 'Bring your brother down'?" Then Judah said to his father Israel, "Send the boy with me, and let us be on our way, so that we may live and not die — you and we and also our little ones. I myself will be surety for him; you can hold me accountable for him. If I do not bring him back to you and set him before you, then let me bear the blame forever. If we had not delayed, we would now have returned twice."

Then their father Israel said to them, "If it must be so, then do this: take some of the choice fruits of the land in your bags, and carry them down as a present to the man — a little balm and a little honey, gum, resin, pistachio nuts, and almonds. Take double the money with you. Carry back with you the money that was returned in the top of your sacks; perhaps it was an oversight. Take your brother also, and be on your way again to the man; may God Almighty grant you mercy before the man, so that he may send back your other brother and Benjamin. As for me, if I am bereaved of my children, I am bereaved" (Genesis 42:35—43:14).

Narrator: The brothers came back to Egypt a second time. *(Brothers enter from back of sanctuary)* They still have not recognized Joseph as their brother. This time they bring along young Benjamin. A testing ensues. Not a teasing nor revenge but a testing of the brothers ten. Is their sorrow and repentance genuine or not?

The brothers are fearful. What intrigue is happening to them? Why money in their sacks of grain? The same money they paid for the grain? They are invited to the banquet in Joseph's house. Let's see what is happening.

(all sit at banquet table)

Joseph: And how is your father?

Gad: Your servant, our father Jacob, is well. He is still alive after all these years.

Joseph: Who is this? *(points to young Benjamin)*

Asher: Why this, your excellency, is our youngest brother, Benjamin. *(Benjamin bows)*

Joseph: God be kind and gracious to you Benjamin.

Benjamin: Thank you, Sir.

Joseph: *(claps hands)* Serve the meal! *(leaves and weeps at stage right)* They're all here! All my brothers. O how I love my little brother Benjamin. How I have missed him. Now here we all are, but I must not cave in. I can't play my hand just yet. Oh, my, they seem repentant. Grown up and mature. It seems they are genuinely sorry for their treatment of me so many years ago. We'll see.

Joseph: *(returns)* Eat up, drink up, enjoy, more food. *(claps hands)*

(music)

Homily Four — Part Two
Genesis 43:29, 30
Family Ties

"Then he looked up and saw his mother's sons and said, 'Is this your youngest brother of whom you spoke to me? God be gracious to you my son!' With that Joseph hurried out, because he was so overcome with affection for his brother and he was about to weep ..." (Genesis 43:29-30).

Joseph plays innocent. He acts as if he doesn't know what's going on. He *is* Joseph — Pharaoh's overseer. He is *not* Jacob's son and brother to the Hebrew brothers.

But his heart is about to burst. His love for Benjamin is overwhelming. He leaves to weep for joy in secret.

There are two families of which you and I are members. There is the human family. There is the spiritual family. Lucky the person that has both. What a tragedy the person who has neither.

The *human family* according to Martin Luther is the highest order in God's creation. Families — however defined — form the bedrock of a healthy society and prosperous nation.

Dolores Curran in her book *Traits of a Healthy Family* identifies fifteen traits that contribute to strong and vibrant family life.

Three of the traits reflect Joseph's deep affection for brother Benjamin.

1. The healthy family communicates.
2. The healthy family plays and laughs together.
3. The healthy family shares a religious core.

1. The healthy family communicates and listens. Earlier Joseph's dysfunctional family of origin spewed hatred and resentment, and spawned secrets and lies. But by inference one can assume that the trait of communication and listening was nurtured by mother Rachel, Joseph, and little Benjamin.

Graduate students at the University of Chicago, when asked where they got their major ideas in morals and religions replied, "Through the conversation in our family at mealtime."

The symbolic center of family life today is no longer the kitchen table but the refrigerator door. On the refrigerator door everyone's schedule and activities are displayed, secured by magnets.

The healthy family resists the refrigerator door and maintains and values table time and table conversation and prayer. The vibrant, closely knit family communicates and listens with respect and love.

2. A second trait in healthy families is a sense of play and laughter together. I love my sister and brothers. One of my lasting memories of our youth is the humor, laughter, and good times we shared. To this day a gesture, a word, a story evokes immediate recognition and hearty guffaws. Family jokes, stories, and comic observations provide the bond that keeps families together.

Joseph's deep attachment and strong affection for his younger brother Benjamin bubbles out almost uncontrollably.

A father promised to take his son fishing one evening after dinner. The phone rang and his business partner requested some time at the office. The father wisely declined and said, "Somebody else can give you input on this, but nobody else can be a father to my son tonight."

3. The healthy family has a shared religious core. Joseph's trust in God and unrelenting love for Benjamin and his bandit brothers reveals a deep religious center. Here true faith is modeled and practiced.

Josh Billings said, "Train up a child in a way he should go — and incidentally walk there yourself once in a while."

Harley Swiggum, founder of the Bethel Bible Studies, said, "One hour in the living room with the parent talking about Christian concepts is worth six years in Sunday school in effectiveness."

I started out this homily by announcing that healthy families have two families. A human family and a spiritual family. Your spiritual family came about by God's grace in action. Your faith family emerged in holy baptism. You received brothers and sisters, a spiritual family in the waters of baptism that connected you to the life, death, and resurrection of Jesus Christ, and in this faith family you are nurtured and fed and grown through word and sacrament.

Tonight, in this intergenerational "Hey Joseph!" Lenten worship, we are happy to affirm family life as we celebrate both our human and spiritual families.

(music)

Repentance Tested
(The Silver Cup Incident)
Genesis 44:1-34

Characters
Genesis Writer
Joseph
Steward
Police
Brothers

Props
Tall, small drafting table, pen with feather, parchment, uniforms for Police, sacks of grain, silver cup (larger than life if possible)

(music)

Scene 1
(Writer is sitting in his studio. He writes a while before speaking)

Genesis Writer: Oh, hello there. I was so engrossed in my writing project here that I almost didn't notice you. Welcome to this Lenten worship. "Hey Joseph!" has been a great series, hasn't it?

You may wonder who I am. I am the one who gathered the stories about Joseph and his brothers and sisters and wrote them down. See my feather pen and my parchment? Had no computer like in your day. I also compiled the entire book of Genesis. So I am the Genesis writer. Some call me Moses and some scholars call me J P and E. Call me what you will. God's Spirit has been with me every step of the way. Boy, has this been an experience.

Let's see where we've been thus far. Hmm. Oh yes, Joseph is now in Egypt. His brothers came to buy grain. You see there was this famine in the land. Joseph had wisely acted under, of course, the command of the Pharaoh. *(pauses)*

Here we are now in Joseph's court. Here are the brothers. *(characters enter, bow, and take their places, standing or on knees)* Now Joseph decides to concoct a bogus crime. *(aside to the audience)* Now when I say crime I suppose every crime fighter in Egypt will appear. Police, detectives, the FBI, the CIA, and the boy scouts. *(rolls his eyes; Police enter and suspiciously look around)* Sure enough, say the word "crime" and there they are. This is what happened:

Joseph: Fill these Canaanites' sacks with food. Fill 'em up. Full. Real full. They need bread for the journey and bread when they get home. *(whispers so that the audience hears but not the Brothers)* Steward, now put this silver cup *(holds it high but not so the Brothers can see it)* in the top of the sack of the youngest. Also, put the money they paid for the grain back in each sack.

Steward: Seems like a strange thing you are doing, Sir.

Joseph: It may seem strange — I have my reasons. Do as I say!

Steward: I will do as you say, Sir. There. Done.

Joseph: Thank you, Steward. *(to the Brothers)* Oh — good-bye, Hebrews. Have a pleasant journey.

Genesis Writer: The brothers headed back for Canaan. *(Brothers walk down the aisle)* But oops — they got just a short distance from the city when Joseph suddenly blurted out ...

Joseph: I've been robbed! Help! Murder! Police! My wife fell in the grease! After them! *(laughs [melodrama music]; Steward and Police run after Brothers and bring them back)*

Police: *(interrogates Brothers as in a police station; may use bright light)* Hey, what is going on here? Look, *here* are the stolen goods! Cup, money, contraband. Caught you red handed!

Thieves. Robbers. Why have you stolen Joseph's silver cup? Why pay evil for good, you good-for-nothings?

(Brothers stammer and try to apologize and explain; freeze)

(music)

Homily Five
Genesis 44:4b
Falsely Accused!

"Why have you stolen my silver cup?" (Genesis 44:4b).

What is happening here? Is Joseph playing a mean trick on his brothers? Is he, like a cat torturing, playing with an exhausted, beleaguered mouse? Why does Joseph *plant* a silver cup in Benjamin's bag and then accuse the brothers of theft?

It appears that Joseph's purpose is to test the genuineness of their repentance. Joseph will not tolerate an easy or cheap repentance!

And so my brothers and sisters in Christ, in this "Hey Joseph!" Lenten series, based on the biblical Joseph from the Bible, we have encountered the experience of "Innocence Accused" once again.

It is a dreadful experience to be accused wrongfully. All of us would avoid like the plague, a situation whereby we are accused of deeds we didn't do.

Joseph was innocently accused himself. Potiphar's wife, that sleazy seductress, made sexual advances and then accused *him* of trying to molest *her*! She succeeded for a time.

However, Joseph maintained his sterling character. He was a man of superior reproach. He refused to walk in moral mud. Joseph would not violate the trust his master Potiphar had given him. Nor would Joseph violate the code of conduct he felt consistent with God's will.

Jesus, in the New Testament was falsely accused. He was accused of blasphemy. Jesus was accused of breaking the law by eating unharvested grain on the sabbath. Jesus was accused of relating to the undesirable of society — prostitutes, tax collectors, and Gentiles.

They conducted three trials to finally sentence Jesus to death. In all of this Jesus was totally and completely innocent.

Isaiah predicted that he would be falsely accused.

Now the brothers ten are innocently accused. They are accused of stealing back their money and robbing Joseph of a silver cup.

Judah, the oldest brother, stands up to confess the collective guilt. Thus the confession of guilt becomes an act of human freedom in responsibility, and in this freedom, the situation in which the brothers have no guilt, they are ready to receive the punishment. But the brothers now understand their father's terrible loss.

How have you felt when you have been unjustly criticized or accused of a misstep even though you were innocent?

(Use your own personal experience) I remember being accused of cheating on a test by my high school English teacher because my grade was the same as the person next to me. I was furious. I darted up to the teacher and bellowed, "I did not cheat on the test!"

How have you felt and what did you do? How did you respond? With anger? With burning resentment?

Just as important is the question, "How have you reacted when you were justly accused of a wrong you were actually responsible for?"

Bennett Cerf in *Laughter, Incorporated* tells Schiller's story about the visit of Emperor Frederick the Great to Potsdam Prison. Each man interviewed proclaimed his complete innocence. They had all been framed. Someone else was to blame. But at last one poor fellow, handing his head, said, "Your Majesty, I am guilty and richly deserve my punishment." Frederick bellowed for the warden: "Come and free this soul! Get him out of here before he corrupts all the whole, innocent souls in this prison!"

The power of the cross of Christ will never be ours until we recognize our need for it.

Paul writes to the Colossians, "And you, who once were estranged and hostile in mind ... he has now reconciled ... by his death" (Colossians 1:21).

So what is this business of planted silver cups and returned money all about? The result of this intrigue is that Judah realizes the collective guilt of his brothers. He realizes the pain his father has gone through. And the brothers start to come to their senses.

(music)

Genesis Writer: Joseph was neither full of revenge nor mean spirited. He simply wanted to test the genuineness of their repentance. He wanted to see if they were truly sorry for their past bad deeds. Let's peek in on the drama again and see what is happening.

(Brothers meekly enter with their closed sacks of grain)

Joseph: What dastardly deed have you done? Let's see your sacks of grain.

(each Brother bows down obediently and open his sack as Police supervise the search)

Brothers: *(one at a time, after opening sack)* Nothing in mine. Mine neither. Nor mine. None here.

Joseph: Take a look in our — er — *your* youngest brother Benjamin's sack.

Brothers: *(smirk and are boastful)* Nothing in Ben's bag. You'll find nothin' there! *(laugh nervously)*

Police: Well what's this? *(shows silver cup)*

Brothers: *(shocked and terribly dismayed, they fall against one another and fall down. All show great consternation)* Oh, no. Not little Bennie's bag! We're toast. *(they tear or throw off their outer clothing)*

Joseph: This deed you have done is inexcusable. *(melodramatic music)* But no problem. *(light happy music)* The one in whom's sack was found the silver cup will simply be my *slave here in Egypt from now on!*

Brothers: *(horrified)* Oh, no. How can we clear Benjamin and ourselves of this mess? We have been guilty of things in the past. Yeah, like selling our brother Joseph to those Ishmaelites. But this smells like a set up.

Judah: *(bows)* Oh, my lord, servant of the most high, Pharaoh, ruler of all Egypt and no doubt esteemed throughout the world, please listen.

Joseph: I'm listening.

Judah: Oh, most esteemed one. Do not be angry.

Joseph: Well I'll get angry if you don't stop slobbering and get to the point. What is it?

Judah: Our dear father, Jacob, is still living.

Joseph: Yes.

Judah: He has one son from his beloved late wife Rachel.

Joseph: Go on.

Judah: He would die if that young son were taken from him. You see he has already lost one son. *(Joseph may look knowingly at the audience)* The silver cup was found in his sack. No denying it. We are sorry. So very, very sorry. We will do *anything* to avoid further pain for our father.

Joseph: Anything?

Judah: Yes, my lord, anything!

Joseph: *(aside to audience)* Something has happened here. *(to Judah)* What do you propose?

Judah: Let *me* remain as a slave to you instead of the young boy. I will be your slave now and from henceforth!

Joseph: All right, we'll see.

Genesis Writer: So the drama goes on. Let's see, I'd better get busy and finish the story. *(starts to write, speaks gleefully)* Wait till you see what happens next week. Till then. *(lights fade)*

(music)

Shalom Restored
Genesis 45:1-20, 25-28

Characters
Announcer
Joseph
Brothers (could be played by one or two who simply change their voices for interest and comic effect)
Pharaoh
Jacob

Props
Live microphones for voices and for sound effects, sound effect equipment as needed for dramatic presentation, tall stools behind each microphone, music stand for each and/or black folders for the scripts

Setting
A live radio show studio with participants standing and wearing earphones at microphones

(music)

Scene 1
Announcer: Good evening ladies and gentlemen. Tonight we present on KMES Radio — our live programming from the old downtown Roxy Theatre. Preeeesseeennnnting "Hey Joseph!" an Old Testament story series original written by Arley K. Fadness and directed by _____. Our characters are

_____.

Tonight, the "Hey Joseph!" drama continues and we will see "Shalom Restored" as the battling brothers come together — finally. We will be amazed to hear Joseph say at long last — *(dramatically)* "I am Joseph, your brother!" *(dramatic music)*

Ladies and gentlemen — a short recap — remember all of you out there in radioland how Joseph had his steward plant the silver cup in Benjamin's sack? He tested his rascal brothers' *repentance* to see if they were truly genuine in their sorrow over what they had done.

Now we open with the scene in which Joseph can no longer contain himself before all those who stood before him and he cries out ...

Joseph: Send everyone away from me! Quickly! Now!

(sound effect: shuffling feet walking away, opening and closing doors)

Announcer: When the brothers and all those had left, Joseph wept loudly.

(Joseph weeps loudly, but seriously, while sad music plays)

Joseph: Now I'm okay. Bring them back in.

(sound effect: doors open, shuffling feet coming back in)

Announcer: At this point, Joseph, whose heart is bursting, finally announces to his brothers:

Joseph: I have something to say to you ...

Brothers: What is it, Sir? Tell us.

Joseph: I am Joseph, your brother!
I am Joseph, your long lost brother!
I am alive. I am Joseph! Remember me?

Brothers: Joseph? *(worried, they stutter and stammer)* You mean ...

Joseph: Come closer. *(removes regal hat; brothers make sounds of oh, ooooh, ah)* See — I am he. I am your brother, Joseph whom you sold into Egypt. Now don't be alarmed or angry with yourselves because you sold me here; for God sent me before you to preserve life — yours and thousands of others.

Brother: What then has been happening these past years ... Sir ... er ... brother Joseph?

Brother: Yes, yes, tell us, brother Joseph, what is going on? We are tooootally confused!

Joseph: Well, after you sold me to the Ishmaelites ... *(music; Joseph talks in low tones to the brothers for about one minute during the music)*

Announcer: Joseph told the brothers the whole story and brought them up to date. They were astonished! *(astonishment music)*

Joseph: Well ... the famine has been here in the land for these last two years and my interpretation of Pharaoh's dream indicates that there will be five more years.

Brother: Oh really?

Brother: How awful!

Brother: What will happen to us?

Brother: How can this be?

Joseph: There will be five more years of neither plowing nor harvesting. But you know what? God sent me here *before* you to preserve for you a remnant on earth and to keep alive for you many survivors.

Brother: So you are not mad?

67

Joseph: No, my brothers, it was not *you* who sent me as a slave — but God — God has made me a father to Pharaoh, and lord of all his house and ruler over all the land of Egypt. Amazing, isn't it?

Now let's go grab a burger and a root beer and I'll tell you more. *(as they leave, they talk and their voices fade away)* What about Dad? And your mothers? Dinah? How are the flocks doing? *(feet shuffling out)*

Announcer: After Joseph and his brothers had taken a break they came back to Joseph's court. The brothers brought in young Benjamin who had been out tending the camels and the donkeys. *(donkey brays)*

(feet shuffling in)

Joseph: Oh, Benjamin! Oh my, oh my! Ben, Ben!

Announcer: When Joseph saw his full brother Benjamin, he ran over and hugged him and kissed him and the two wept. *(ad lib reunion talk through tears)*

They then had a long talk about their Dad, the flocks back home, and many things.

(sentimental music)

Homily Six — Part One
Genesis 45:5b, 7, 8
Bad Fortunes; Good Results

"... God sent me before you to preserve life ... and to keep alive for you many survivors. It was not you who sent me here, but God ..." (Genesis 45:5b, 7, 8).

There has been little else on people's minds the summer of 2004 than the devastating hurricanes that cruised through Florida and the southern and eastern seaboards of the United States.

The Atlantic hurricane season came with innocuous names like Alex, Bonnie, Charley, Danielle, Earl, Frances, Gaston, Hermine,

Ivan (twice — came back as tropical depression #10), Jeanne, Karl, Lisa, Matthew, Nicole, Otto, Paula, Richard, Shary, Tomas, Virginie, and Walter. Sounding like a pleasant family of siblings, cousins, aunts and uncles, they came with relentless force like a swarm of hostile hornets one after another.

Hurricanes come with such angry fury — trashing towns, flattening orange groves, smashing beach homes and inland businesses, taking lives and injuring thousands. Yet even thousands more survived and thanked God for their deliverance that appeared to them to be providential.

How ironic and timely is this for our text. Speaking of Joseph as he speaks to his nervous brothers, " ... God sent me before you to preserve life ... and to keep alive for you many survivors. It was not you who sent me here, but God...."

It's a great thing when God sends someone to preserve life. It may be governmental agencies; the state governor; the National Guard; county, state, and national systems; the Red Cross; Lutheran Social Services, or the Salvation Army.

It's a great thing when churches and people like you and me feel commissioned by God "to preserve life and to keep alive many survivors."

Now to the *untrained* eye the story of Joseph is a storybook tale of happy endings. Everything turns out right in the end. And they all lived happily ever after.

But to the *trained* eye and to the heart that is in tune, the story of Joseph is a testimony of faith and trust in God. It is not a rags to riches Horatio Alger story but a hope-filled and positive assessment of the whole tawdry affair which began with the gift of the coat of many colors.

We admire two things. Joseph's *optimism* and Joseph's *hope*.

1. First Joseph's *optimism*. Someone has said, "Optimism is a cheerful frame of mind that enables a teakettle to sing, though in hot water up to its nose."

The optimist fell ten stories,
And at each window bar
He shouted to the folks inside:
"Doing all right so far!"

69

Twixt optimist and pessimist
The difference is droll:
The optimist sees the doughnut;
The pessimist sees the hole.

A pastor who lived in Chicago, his hometown, saw a bunch of children playing baseball. He asked one of the boys how the game was going. The boy said, "145 to nothing!" The pastor asked, "Whose favor?" The boy pointed to the team at bat and said "Theirs." The pastor said, "They're beating you pretty badly aren't they?" The boy looked up and said, "I don't know, we ain't been up to bat yet." (source unknown)

Is your cup half full or half empty? Joseph's cup appears half full. The Bible has no record of Joseph's anger, resentment, or cynicism.

2. Now secondly — and more important than optimism — Joseph had *hope*. Hope is optimistic but it is not the same as a cheery optimism. A painted smile, a contrived "Have a nice day!" is not the same as hope.

Hope is rooted in God's ultimate will. Hope springs from God at work in the world and in one's life.

Hope believes "with God all things are possible." Hope sings, "Lord God! Behold you have made the heavens and the earth by your great power and outstretched arm, and there is nothing too hard for you."

Hope blossoms. Paul said it; you and I can believe it: "I can do all things through Christ who strengthens me."

"Fear not, for I am with you. Be not dismayed; for I am your God. I will strengthen you, yes I will help you."

Joseph full of hope and godly optimism says to his brothers, "It was not you who sent me but God."

Can you feel the finger of God tap you on the shoulder tonight? God calls you and me to preserve life as Joseph preserved life and kept alive many survivors.

It is in a very concrete way that we can help starting now. In the Sudan, in Haiti, in urban neighborhoods, in rural America, next door. We reach out and make good results from bad fortunes.

(music)

Scene 2

Announcer: When the announcement was made in Pharaoh's palace, "Joseph's brothers have come," Pharaoh and his servants were pleased. *(laughter, pleasant conversation)*
  Pharaoh said to Joseph:

Pharaoh: Say to your brothers, Joseph, "Do this: load your animals and go back to the land of Canaan. Bring your aged father, Jacob, back with you and all of your households and come so that I may give you the very best Egypt has to offer."

Announcer: And Joseph said:

Joseph: Oh, my, that would be wonderful!

Announcer: And furthermore, Pharaoh said:

Pharaoh: You are further commanded to take wagons from Egypt for your children and those who need a ride such as the women and aged as your father Jacob and bring them in comfort. It is a long way to travel.

Joseph: Oh, thank you, your eminence.

Pharaoh: Bring everything you want, but do not worry about possessions. My land, Egypt, is at your disposal.

Announcer: The brothers and their companions did what Pharaoh commanded. They were delighted and soon the wagons were traveling. *(wagon travel sounds, shuffling of feet, crowd noises)* When they got to Canaan, they made the announcement to their dad.

Brothers: Dad, Dad!

Jacob: Welcome back, boys. I've been lonesome for you. Did you have a good trip?

Brothers: We're glad to be back, too, but you know what ...

Jacob: Hey what is it with all the extra goods and grain?

Brothers: You'll never believe it Dad but it's true ...

Jacob: What's true? Speak up. Don't keep an old man guessing.

Brother: It's Joseph!

Jacob: Who?

Brothers: It's Joseph!

Jacob: Joseph? *(dramatic music)* My dead son? *(dramatic music)*

Brothers: Yes — we mean no!

Jacob: Yes — No, what do you mean? Don't play riddles with me. Joseph who?

Brothers: Joseph! Your long lost son, our brother, is alive!

Jacob: Don't fool with me, sons. I'm too old for mind games.

Brothers: No, no it's true. Joseph is alive. He is a ruler in Pharaoh's Egypt where we sold him years and years ago. And he sends for *you* — dearest father.

Jacob: You sold him? He's not dead! Why — ohhh-ohhhh!

Announcer: It took a while but Jacob finally comprehended the reality of Joseph being alive. After some time absorbing the news, the entire family packed up and in a short while were on their way to the land of Egypt.

(traveling sounds)

Announcer: The reunion was wonderful. When Jacob saw his beloved Joseph after all these years he was overcome with emotion. Joseph, too, wept like he had never wept before.

Joseph: Oh, dearest father, I have waited for a long time for this.

Jacob: And oh, how I love you Joseph, son of my wonderful wife Rachel.

Joseph: Lots of strange things happened to me, father Jacob, but God sent me before you to preserve life. It was not my brothers who brought me here but God did and God did for a purpose — a marvelous purpose to benefit all God's people! Now let's enjoy one another and celebrate!

(music)

Homily Six — Part Two
Genesis 50:19-21
Shalom Restored
(The Healing Of The Family)

"Joseph said to them, 'Do not be afraid! Am I in the place of God? Even though you intended to do harm to me, God intended it for good, in order to preserve a numerous people, as he is doing today. So have no fear; I myself will provide for your little ones' " (Genesis 50:19-21).

We come to the end of the marvelous story of Joseph and his brothers. The family is finally reunited. The family of Jacob is preserved. Shalom is re-established. There is forgiveness and trust and unity and peace. And from this family God will bring forth a special nation — the nation of Israel with its twelve tribes named after the twelve sons and their descendants.

Claus Westermann, in his book *Joseph*, quotes the Old Testament scholar Von Rad: "Here Joseph finally speaks openly of God, and here the last veil is lifted ... here is the principle theme of the entire story: The hand of God, which describes to lead to a gracious end — ends all the confusions of human guilt. Joseph wishes to concentrate all attention on that which is most important: the leading of God, which had made use of all of these dark things for good."[1]

"The human mind plans the way, but the Lord directs the steps" (Proverbs 16:9).

"All our steps are ordered by the Lord; how then can we understand our own ways?" (Proverbs 20:24).

It is a great and wonderful work of God to see broken families reunited and healed.

It is my prayer that your family, too, may be healed through the re-establishment of trust, forgiveness, communication, respect, and above all sincere love.

Amen.

(music)

---

1. Claus Westermann, *Joseph: Eleven Bible Stories on Genesis* (Minneapolis: Fortress Press, 1993), p. 96.

Maundy Thursday
Lord's Supper — Living Tableau

Prelude   "Sweet Hour Of Prayer"
                                "When I Survey The Wondrous Cross"

Song   "Joseph's Dream"
Used by permission John Ylvisaker, Waverly, Iowa

Monologue by Joseph

Welcome Monologue by Mary Magdala

Responsive Reading   Psalm 51:1-13
Leader: Have mercy on me, O God, according to your steadfast
         love; according to your abundant mercy blot out my
         transgressions.
**All: Wash me thoroughly from my iniquity, and cleanse
         me from my sin.**
Leader: For I know my transgressions, and my sin is ever before
         me.
**All: Against you, you alone, have I sinned, and done what
         is evil in your sight, so that you are justified in your
         sentence and blameless when you pass judgment.**
Leader: Indeed, I was born guilty, a sinner when my mother con-
         ceived me.
**All: You desire truth in the inward being; therefore teach
         me wisdom in my secret heart.**
Leader: Purge me with hyssop, and I shall be clean; wash me,
         and I shall be whiter than snow.
**All: Let me hear joy and gladness; let the bones that you
         have crushed rejoice.**
Leader: Hide your face from my sins, and blot out all my iniquities.

75

All: **Create in me a clean heart, O God, and put a new and right spirit within me.**

Leader: Do not cast me away from your presence, and do not take your Holy Spirit from me.

All: **Restore to me the joy of your salvation, and sustain in me a willing spirit.**

Leader: Then I will teach transgressors your ways, and sinners will return to you.

Lenten Hymn   "When Israel Was In Egypt's Land"

Meditation   "Jesus, Bread Of Life"

Confession Of Sins

Personal Absolution
(Worshipers come forward and receive the laying on of hands. Respond with "Amen")

Nicene Creed

Offering   "I Don't Know How To Love Him"

Introduction by Martha Of Bethany

Song   "Gathering The Disciples"

Monologue by Mary, The Mother Of Jesus

Jesus Washes His Disciples' Feet
(Organ Interlude)   "Meditation #3"
Judas Exits

Words Of Institution

Lord's Prayer

Distribution Of Holy Communion

Hymn   "Blessed Assurance"

Blessing
Our crucified and risen Lord, Jesus Christ, who now hath bestowed upon you his holy body and blood, whereby he hath made full satisfaction for all your sins, strengthen and preserve you in the true faith into everlasting life. Peace be with you. Amen.

Narration by Lydia and Priscilla

Post Communion Canticle "Hallelujah! We Sing Your Praises"

Prayer

Benediction

Dismissal

Postlude   "The Penitent Heart"

Jesus, Bread Of Life

John 6:35, 41, 48, 50, 51, 58

"I am the Bread of Life" — Jesus
There it sits.
Golden brown. Unsliced.
Basted with butter.
Glistening and proud.
Hot right from Mother's oven.

Yum, yum. Oh, how we lusted after Mom's freshly baked bread. Her loaves were gorgeous. You could smell the aroma waft it's way down the path.

"Time for supper!"

We sat down — mumbled a prayer and then dove in like pigs. "Pass the bread!" We sliced it. Heaped mounds of strawberry jam and chokecherry jelly on each slice. Sometimes we smothered Mom's bread in homemade peanut butter. Dad looked on proudly as he munched his slice knowing it was made from wheat grown in his own field in the south forty.

Mother's bread. I can still feel it and taste it and smell it. Better than grocery bread by a long shot. She baked all kinds: Raisin bread, rye bread, wheat bread, oat bread, french bread, banana bread, sour bread, date bread, flat bread, and fruit bread.

You know, tonight I wish Mom was able to bake *one more loaf.* She wishes she could, too. But now and for tonight the memory and image will do.

Bread is basic to life. Bread is symbolic of all the food we eat. "Give us our daily bread," Jesus taught his disciples to pray.

Martin Luther expands the meaning of "bread": "Daily bread includes everything needed for this life, such as food and clothing, home and property, work and income, good government, favorable weather, peace and health, a good name, and true friends and neighbors" (Luther's *Small Catechism*).

In our "Hey Joseph!" Lenten series, Joseph, God's man for the hour, walks out of the Old Testament and into our sanctuary to tell us and to show us how he was used by God to save life. Joseph

79

fed not only his loved ones — Jacob's family — but the Egyptians as well, and he ensured the future of the nation Israel. Joseph becomes a type — a prototype of God's Messiah who would come.

Later in the wilderness, God fed the Israelites with manna. A miraculous gift from heaven.

In John 6, Jesus reveals to his listeners who he is and what his purpose is. "I am the bread of Life" he tells them. Six times in six verses Jesus refers to himself as the bread sent down from heaven. He, like manna, is from God and for the people.

But many take offense at him. They explode in anger! This cannot be! They reject Jesus' words. They reject Jesus himself. They reject nourishment, strength, health, energy, life, and power.

Jesus demonstrates not only in words but in visible tangible form to all who believe in his offering. "This bread is my body. This wine is my blood. Take and eat. Take and drink."

"For in doing so," said the Apostle Paul, "you proclaim the Lord's death until he comes again."

Are you hungry? Feeling weak, empty, lonely? Unsure and unsteady?

Look, my brothers and sisters, at the loaf again.

The loaf is large. It is no temporary manna in the wilderness. It is no little, bitty bun. It is so large and so comprehensive that you and I will never ever hunger again. It is a loaf that will satisfy you forever.

"O taste and see," said the psalmist, "see that the Lord is good" (Psalm 34:8a).

Joseph's Monologue

Note: Joseph is in costume. This monologue is memorized. The props of the "Hey Joseph!" series are gone. He may speak from the center of the congregation or to the side of the Lord's Supper backdrop scene when that is used.

Good evening. I am Joseph, son of Jacob and Rachel, brother to Judah, Zebulun, Gad, Issachar, Reuben, Levi, Simeon, Benjamin, my youngest beloved brother, Asher, Naphatali, and Dan.

These past forty days in your Lenten season you have gathered faithfully to help me relive my story. "Hey Joseph!" you called it. Thanks for a great time and experience together.

Now your focus is not on me, but on Jesus of Nazareth. He is my Savior and yours. They said of me that I and my experiences paralleled many experiences of Jesus, too. I am humbled by the comparison. But he must increase. I must decrease.

- As I was innocently accused of a crime I didn't commit with Potiphar's wife, so Jesus was accused of blasphemy, consorting with sinners, and a lot of trumped up charges. I lived. Jesus died.
- I resisted temptation and evil. So did Jesus, God's Son who defeated the devil in the wilderness.
- I harbored no revenge in my heart against my bandit brothers. Jesus went way beyond that — he loved and forgave even his tormentors.
- I was a key player in bringing back shalom and reconciliation to my family. Jesus' entire life, death, and resurrection brought reconciliation to the whole world.
- I provided bread in a time of famine. Jesus not only provides bread for a hungry world — Jesus is the Bread of Life. So tonight welcome and worship.

Mary Of Magdala's Monologue

Good evening, I am Mary from Magdala. Four other women from the Bible — Martha from Bethany, Mary, the mother of Jesus, Lydia, and Priscilla, and I will serve as your hostesses and worship leaders in the celebration of Holy Communion. Before you is the Upper Room and soon Jesus and his twelve disciples will gather there and we will celebrate the holy meal together.

They called me Mary Magdalene since I came from that region in Palestine — Magdala. It's on the southwest coast of the Sea of Galilee.

I first met Jesus when I really needed help. Seven evil spirits seemed to dominate my life. Jesus touched me and cast the demons out. I remember shouting, "Now I'm free! Thanks be to God."

I followed Jesus in his early Galilean ministry with Joanna, Susanna, and others. I contributed financially to Jesus' venture. It was hard but I followed him to Jerusalem. I was present at the horrible crucifixion. Later I saw the empty tomb and was thrilled to see him alive again! Harlot I am not, as some labeled me. A credible witness of the Savior, I believe I am.

It was in this very Upper Room (motions to the Upper Room scene) prepared for the Passover Feast where the Master repeated the Great Commandment. You remember it. "Love one another even as I have loved you." Jesus then demonstrated that love by washing his disciples' feet and then instituting the Lord's Supper.

As you Christians reflect on how Joseph in the Old Testament was the bread provider in a time of famine, so now meditate on Christ as the Bread of Life in this famine of sin and brokenness. You celebrate in faith — Jesus' true presence in the bread and wine in this his Holy Sacrament.

But first let us prepare our hearts by beginning worship. Turn to King David's great Psalm of contrition and confession — Psalm 51, verses 1-13.

Martha Of Bethany's Monologue

Hello.

My name is Martha. I'm the sister of another Mary. She's not here tonight. My brother was Lazarus. Remember us? We lived in Bethany and many times Jesus visited us.

I was in charge of our household and served Jesus when he would drop by for a visit. I'd make him a lunch. Once, I was busy in the kitchen and grew very impatient with my sister Mary, for her doting on Jesus' little homilies. But afterward, Jesus spoke to me and I realized I was too involved with lesser things.

Yet they say I was a true follower of Jesus. When my brother Lazarus died and my sister was practically paralyzed with grief, I got up and went out to meet Jesus as he came down the road to Bethany.

I served Jesus and his disciples many times for dinner and for other needs they had. Later on, Jesus, this very same Jesus whom I served food and drink, would announce to me and to the multitudes that he was the Bread of Life.

Jesus loved all three of us so deeply. He even healed people like Simon the leper right in my home.

Your tradition says I was a follower all right, even though at times I concentrated too much on secondary things. But I did my best, and I believe God our Creator was honored.

I was around when Jesus began to call his women and men, too, to follow him. He gathered twelve special people as his disciples and they joined him at that last Passover Supper.

Mary, The Mother Of Jesus' Monologue

My name is Mary. I am the mother of Jesus. You know me. You know me so well. I'm thankful and grateful and so humbled that God used me as a simple handmaiden to bring salvation to the world.

I raised my son in his childhood and I followed him in his adult life. Many times I was filled with joy and many times I was perplexed.

My Son, Jesus, confused me that time in the temple when he was twelve years old and then later at the wedding at Cana — at times I felt anxious and worried — more often though I felt peace and calm from my God.

But the time that hurt so much was when I had to stand at the foot of the cross and see him tortured, dying — only 33 — so young — and I heard him tell John to take care of me. What a son — what a loss — I was so sorry — yet I knew in my heart something was coming.

I remembered the passage in Isaiah 61, when the prophet said, "... he has sent me to bring good news to the oppressed, to bind up the brokenhearted and to proclaim liberty to the captives ..." and then when God raised him from the dead I knew my son was the good news.

Watch now with me my sisters and brothers, how he demonstrates the Great Commandment to love one another, by washing his disciple's feet in that Upper Room.

(Jesus washes the disciples' feet; musical background)

(Judas leaves)

Oh look at him go. Judas Iscariot had made evil plans to betray Jesus to the Jews — he now knows it is time.

After Jesus washed his disciples' feet, he began to speak:

(Pastor speaks the Words Of Institution and leads in the Lord's Prayer)

84

Lydia And Priscilla's Monologue

Lydia: When everyone had communed at that first Lord's Supper, they knew that they had proclaimed the Lord's death. They knew that this was the first installment of a wonderful banquet that would go on for centuries.

I'm Lydia and this is Priscilla.

Priscilla: Hello everyone. I'm so happy to be here and worship with you — this is truly a wonderful night. I pray God's blessings upon us all.

Lydia: We celebrated the Lord's Supper in my home, too. My home in Thyatira was the first Christian meeting place years after Jesus ascended.

The Apostle Paul stayed with us for a time. I am known as the woman who sold purple-dyed goods. It was wonderful to have the first Christians meet and worship in my home. I am amazed that we who sat around the table and ate and drank would hear Jesus teach that he was the Bread of Life for us and the world.

Priscilla: I was a leader in the new church, too. I was a tentmaker and teacher with my husband Aquilla. We worked when the church was yet so small in Corinth and Ephesus and Rome, and now the Body of Christ has grown to millions. It has grown because the Holy Spirit has taught its followers love to God and love to one another.

The disciples you see up front are sitting there not because of privilege or status but because they were called to love and to witness. Their stewardship of love and life required the ultimate sacrifice — all but one would give their life in martyrdom.

Lydia: God calls you tonight, too, to eat and drink the words and Bread of Life and then to say words and do deeds of love. Pray the Holy Spirit to lead and guide you to that end.

Jesus, Our Shalom
Ephesians 2:13-14

"But now in Christ Jesus you who once were far off have been brought near by the blood of Christ. For he is our peace ..." (Ephesians 2:13-14).

In a few moments through word and song, we re-live Jesus' last six hours. It was a reluctant Pilate who finally caved in. Loud shouting chief priests insisted and persisted. Certain Jews were convinced it was blasphemous for anyone to claim to be the Son of God. Such a person must die.

So it was not "business as usual" for six hours. "Far worse than the breaking of his body is the shredding of his heart. His own countrymen clamored for his demise. His own disciple planted the kiss of betrayal. His own friends ran for cover. And now his own heavenly Father turns his back on him leaving him alone."

One may ask, "Jesus do you give no thought to saving yourself? What keeps you there? What holds you to the cross? Nails don't hold gods to trees. What makes you stay?"[1]

What makes you stay?

1. His reply is, "I am your shalom." Paul put it this way: "But now in Christ Jesus you who once were far off have been brought near by the blood of Christ. For he is our peace ..." (Ephesians 2:13). There was no shalom. No peace. The dividing walls of hostility were high: between God and Adam; between Cain and Abel; between Joseph and his brothers; and between families, races, nationalities, and cultures. The dividing wall of sin was so high no one could climb over it or under it or around it.

The dividing wall had to be broken down. And a bridge built out of the rubble.

Jesus must do that. He must build shalom. Reconciliation. Peace. God to people. People to God and neighbor to neighbor.

It was through suffering that Jesus brought down the walls and ripped away the fences of division and hostililty.

The writer to the Hebrews wrote: "During the days of Jesus' life on earth, he offered up prayers and petitions with loud cries and tears to the one who could save him from death and he was heard because of his reverent submission. Although he was a son he learned obedience from what he suffered" (Hebrews 5:7-8).

Professor Walter Bruggeman said in a preaching series, "truth most often comes through pain." I surely am not attracted to *that* idea. But upon reflection I must admit it is true — that truth comes through pain.

One can either *loathe* pain or *learn* from it. A. W. Tozer said, "It's doubtful whether God can bless a person greatly until He has hurt him deeply." I don't attribute pain to God but I affirm God's use of difficulty to open us up to faith and trust.

Joseph *suffered* the pain of slavery when his brothers sold him. Joseph *suffered* separation from his father and family. Joseph *suffered* punishment because of false charges brought against him. At the end however, Joseph could say to those of his flesh who failed him, "You intended to harm me, but God intended it for good to accomplish what is now being done, the saving of many lives" (Genesis 50:20).

Through suffering Jesus brings shalom.

2. The second answer to, "what made Jesus stay on the cross," was that by death Jesus slays death.

"Death. Death is the bully on the block. He catches you in the alley. He taunts you in the playground. He badgers you on the way home: 'You too will die someday.' You see him as he escorts the procession of hearse-led cars."[2]

He stands near the intensive care unit. He jabs you. "Your time is coming."

"Oh, we try to prove him wrong. We jog. We diet. We pump iron. We play golf. We try to escape it, knowing all along that we can at best postpone it."[3]

His goal is to "make you and me so afraid of dying that we can never learn to live. He'll steal the joy of your youth and the peace of your final years."[4] So we don't face him alone. The bully is too big to fight by yourself. You need a big brother. "Jesus unmasked death and exposed him for who he really is — a 98-pound weakling dressed up in a Charles Atlas suit."[5]

Johann Sebastian Bach wrote with good intentions, "Come Sweet Death." But the Apostle Paul was by far the better theologian when he called death — in 1 Corinthians 15 — the last enemy to be destroyed! Death is no friend.

We live in a death culture. Many bless Dr. Death who assists suicides in the name of compassion. We have an ever-expanding euthanasia movement. Convenience abortion abounds. Road rage threatens. Tornadoes and hurricanes strike without warning. Shootings in schools continue to occur.

It is true we all will die. But Jesus' death slays the permanence of death. Jesus gives life eternal by his grace to all who believe.

Michael Guido tells in his column *Seeds From The Sower* that when Lincoln's body was brought from Washington to Illinois for burial, it was taken through Albany. In the crowd was a mother and her boy. Raising him above her head, she shouted, "Son, take a good look at that man. He died for you."

On this bad Friday that we call good — take a good look at Jesus. He died for us. He is our peace. He slayed death by his death and by what happened on Easter morn.

More about that on another day.

---

1. Max Lucado, *Six Hours One Friday*, Multnomah Books, p. 20.

2. *Ibid.*, p. 131.

3. *Ibid.*, p. 131.

4. *Ibid.*, p. 131.

5. *Ibid.*, p. 132.

Joseph And Mary In The Garden
John 20:1-18

Characters
> Joseph Of Arimathea
> Mary Magdalene
> Evil Spirit

Props
> Appropriate costumes for the characters

Setting
> In the garden near Joseph of Arimathea's tomb

(Joseph of Arimathea is standing in the garden near the tomb with its stone rolled away)

Joseph: Good morning. I am Joseph. Not the Genesis Joseph who visited you in your Lenten series this year. Nor am I Joseph, the husband of Mary, stepfather of our Lord.

They called me Joseph of Arimathea. I was from the town of Arimathea once called Ramah. I am a member of the Sanhedrin. I objected to the decision by the Sanhedrin to put Jesus to death. I was a secret believer in this Jesus of Nazareth. I was fearful of making my allegiance to Jesus public. But I was compelled to be more courageous when I saw what they did to Jesus. When I saw the crucifixion last Friday, a part of me died right there, too. It was horrible. And the weeping and wailing of the women who loved him so stabbed my soul.

So the least I could do was to go to Pilate and beg for the body of Jesus. I didn't want them to throw him into a burial pit like a dog. Governor Pilate agreed. I took his body to my personal tomb right here in this garden cemetery. I had this tomb hewn out of this rock for me. I was glad to offer it for him. But now I am really confused. They say his body is gone! The guards were speechless. Oh, here's one of the women.

(to Mary Magdalene) Hello!

Mary Magdalene: Oh, hello yourself. Who are you?

Joseph: Joseph. Joseph of Arimathea. I'm a member of the Sanhedrin.

Mary: Oh. You're the one. This is *your* tomb where they laid the body of Jesus.

Joseph: Yes.

Mary: Oh, thank you so much, but ...

Joseph: But what?

Mary: His body is gone!

Joseph: I know. I can't understand it.

Mary: Three of us Marys were at the cross when Jesus died.

Joseph: Three of you Marys?

Mary: Yes, Jesus' *mother Mary*, Jesus' *Aunt Mary of Clopas*, and me, *Mary Magdalene*.

Joseph: Well, I just can't understand it. Jesus' body is gone.

Mary: I know. Could it be?

Joseph: Could it be what?

Mary: Aah, I was just thinking ...

Joseph: Thinking?

Mary: Well, I just talked to what I thought was the gardener, but ...

Joseph: But what, Mary Magdalene?

Mary: It was he!

Joseph: Jesus? Really?

Mary: *(quietly)* Yes, it was Jesus. As alive as you and me.

Joseph: Oh, my!

Mary: Yes.

(a noise is heard in the bushes nearby; a man dressed like a villain in a melodrama leaps out)

Evil Spirit: Ha, Ha! I'm back!

Mary: Pay no attention to him, Joseph.

Joseph: Who is he? Shall I call one of the guards that was here a while ago?

Mary: No, no. I'll deal with him.

Evil Spirit: I'm back. Heh, heh.

Mary: What you see is not real. He's a fake. He's a mirage. He is powerless. He is one of the seven evil spirits Jesus cast out of *me* back when I first met Jesus.

Joseph: I'll get my sword.

Mary: Never mind. *(to Evil Spirit)* Get out of here, you wisp of smoke. You're no longer anything.

Evil Spirit: Oh, yes, I can still make you doubt.

Mary: Doubt?

Evil Spirit: Yes — doubt what you're just starting to believe.

Mary: You mean that Jesus is actually alive?

Evil Spirit: They stole his body. It's somewhere.

Mary: So you think you still have power to make us doubt? Get out of here!

(Evil Spirit disappears)

Mary: *(to Joseph)* He's gone. At least for now.

Joseph: Thank goodness. I almost believed him for a moment!

Mary: I know. He'll be back. Relentless. Dogged. Persistent. But ... oh, somebody's coming ... I wonder who it is?

Joseph: Could it be?

Mary: Oh....

(lights out)

I'm Alive
John 20:1-18

On February 27, 1991, Ruth Dillow was at her home in Chute, Kansas, when she received the news from the Pentagon that her son, PFC Clayton Carpenter had stepped on a land mine in the Persian Gulf and was dead. Ruth was stricken as if a knife had been thrust into her own heart. She heard what no parent ever wants to hear of his/her child.

Three days later, Ruth got another telephone call, and the voice on the other end said, "Mom, I'm alive!"

Ruth said, at first she could not believe it was the voice of her twenty-year-old son, over whom she had mourned for nearly three days. She said, "I jumped up and down! I was overjoyed! You just don't know now much!" (Source unknown)

Mom, I'm alive!

It was said in the garden on Easter morning, too.

"Mother Mary, I, your son, Jesus, am alive."

"Joanna. I, Jesus, am alive."

"Mary Magdala, I'm alive."

"You, the other Mary, mother of James, I'm alive."

"Salome, I'm alive."

"Susanna, I'm alive."

"Mr. Gardener, I'm alive."

"Terrified soldiers, I'm alive."

"You Doubting Thomas, I'm alive."

"Pastor _____, I'm alive. Organist _____, I'm alive. Ushers, I'm alive."

"Children, moms, dads, grandparents, visitors, members, worshipers on this Easter morning, I'm alive!"

It's been a great morning! I love Easter.

This morning I am going to borrow our choir director's baton and conduct an Easter symphony. Did you know that I am a symphony director? When did I conduct my very first symphony? Today. This morning. It is the Symphony of Easter and I invite you to participate. It is the Symphonic Gospel of Jesus Christ. It is beautiful. It is harmonious. It is so powerful it stimulates and recreates our everlasting hope.

My Symphonic Sermon of Salvation has five parts. Five movements. Your part:

The Tomb Is Empty! (right section)

He Is Not Here! (right center)

Christ Has Risen! (left center)

He Has Risen Indeed! (left section)

Hallelujah! (All)

1. The Tomb Is Empty! *(Say it with me; left section)* The first movement of the symphony sets the stage for all that follows. Nothing left but burial clothes. No body. Unlike King David who still lies in his grave in Palestine, Jesus does not. The Tomb Is Empty! It was not enough that the disciple's plans and expectation of Jesus was dashed. Now even in death their expectations evaporate. Why? (Ready?) The Tomb Is Empty!

2. The second movement trumpets He Is Not Here! That's what the angel said in Luke's Gospel. He Is Not Here! *(rehearse two times)* It was an angel who said, "He Is Not Here!" A messenger of God, one sent from God to earth with a message of God's will and plan for our rescue. It seems every time God wants to take another step toward reconciling us to God, God sends an angel — a messenger — to announce it. This one announced: He Is Not Here! As if to say I already know what you're going to do, God knows, God does it: He Is Not Here! And Mary Magdalene confused as to where Jesus was, nevertheless knew two things: The Tomb Is Empty! He Is Not Here!

3. The third movement of our Easter Symphony is Christ Has Risen! Unheard of. Impossible. Incredible. The crucified Lord now lives again. He speaks, "I'm Alive!"

It was Easter morning a couple of years ago when just before the Sunrise Worship a bulletin blooper was discovered. In the hymn "Hallelujah, Jesus Lives," the typist mistyped "Hallelujah, Jesus lives. He is *not* the living one." The pastor had his young daughter go through every bulletin and change the "He is *not* the Living One" to "He is *now* the Living One."

The disciples reeled with seeing the *not* changed to *now*. Dead is dead — isn't it? And yet, the angel's words rang in their heads, Christ Is Risen!

The Symphonic Sermon of Salvation has progressed from the hopelessness of The Tomb Is Empty! through the message that He Is Not Here! to this amazing word: Christ Has Risen!

The harmony and the blending of the symphony begins to take shape. Our voices began to swell with the angel's chorus proclaiming the awesome wonder of our God: The Tomb Is Empty! He Is Not Here! Christ Has Risen!

4. The fourth movement: He Has Risen Indeed! *(congregation practices it)* With believing hearts join the symphony in proclaiming: He Has Risen Indeed! What beauty! What harmony! What symphony! Know this, by faith and baptism into Christ, salvation is yours.

The Tomb Is Empty! He Is Not Here! Christ Is Risen! He Has Risen Indeed!

5. What is left to be said? The fifth movement is a single word — Hallelujah! *(practice it)* Churchy sounding word. Only place we use it is at church. It means: Tah dah! I'm alive, Mom. Horray! Yahoo! Whoopee, Cool, Right on Dudes, Kowabunga, You Betcha, Yada Yada! all wrapped up in one word — Hallelujah!

The Tomb Is Empty! He Is Not Here! Christ Has Risen! He Has Risen Indeed! Hallelujah!

This is our symphony. Our song. Other symphonies are beautiful melodious, commanding, and exciting, but this is authentically the symphony for all of creation for ever and ever. Add your voice to the harmony.

It is told of Johann Sebastian Bach that he was a very sound sleeper. It was difficult to wake him from a nap, but his children discovered a way to do it. They would play a familiar line of music on the piano, but omit the last note. Always, Bach would wake up, go over to the piano, and play the final note. He couldn't stand to have a line of music unfinished. God played the final note of Christ's victory by raising him from the dead.

Dr. Gerhard Frost, late professor at Luther Seminary, wrote a piece of poetry about the resurrection. He ends it by saying, "It had better be true." A pastor student of Dr. Frost, spoke those words at the death of Gerhard's two sisters who were members of the same parish. When sister Florence died, the pastor stood by her casket and quoted her brother, "It had better be true." When Esther Frost died, the pastor again said the same of the resurrection, "It had better be true."

"A pastor in Portland, Oregon, was told by his doctor that he had a terminal illness. On his way home from the clinic, he decided he would drive out of the city. He drove out to the Columbia River where he could see Mount Hood. He sat in his car and wept. Then he stepped out of his car, looked up at the mountain and said, 'Oh, mountain, you have sat there for millennia, and you will stand there thousands more years. But when you are gone, I shall still be alive.'

"Then he looked down at the mighty Columbia River and said, 'Oh, river, you have been running through this valley for thousands of years. But one day you will run dry, but I shall still be alive.' His sadness left. His spirit soared" (Source: Pastor Harold Grindal).

The Tomb Is Empty! He Is Not Here! Christ Has Risen! He Has Risen Indeed! Hallelujah!

Amen.

One Heart Beat

Three days the body lay dead.
72 hours unmoved and cold.
4,320 minutes
the world was silent in that tomb.
259,200 seconds,
not a sound, not a movement.
Creation waiting.
Angels watched anticipating.
Demons watched speculating.
Silence.
One beat!
It shook the room.
Demons fled.
Angels cheered.
One beat!
The victory won.
One beat!
The enemy cursed.
One beat!
The bondage of death broken through.
One beat!
The fulfillment of life.
One beat!
Halleluia!
One beat!
Our hope secured.
One beat!
He lives!
One beat!
Forever!
One beat!
Almighty!
One beat!
Jehovah God!

(Source unknown)

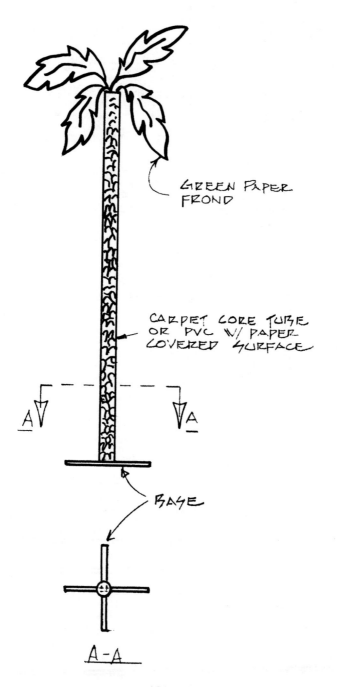

GREEN PAPER
FROND

CARPET CORE TUBE
OR PVC W/ PAPER
COVERED SURFACE

A▽ ▽A

BASE

A-A

101

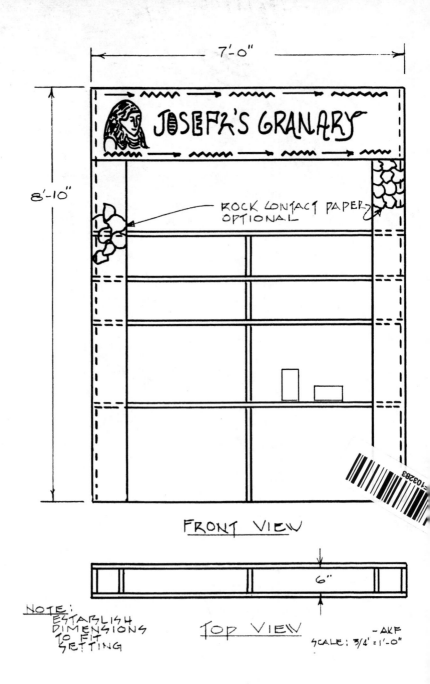

JOSEFA'S GRANARY

ROCK CONTACT PAPER OPTIONAL

7'-0"

8'-10"

FRONT VIEW

6"

TOP VIEW

NOTE:
ESTABLISH
DIMENSIONS
TO FIT
SETTING

SCALE: 3/4' = 1'-0"

- AKF

102